Contents

FAME

FORTUNES, FAILURE AND FAITH

GREG LAURIE
MARSHALL TERRILL

harvest ministries
Riverside, California

FAME: FORTUNES, FAILURE AND FAITH

By GREG LAURIE & MARSHALL TERRILL

Trade Paperback ISBN-13: 978-1-61754-017-2

ebook ISBN-13: 978-1-61754-019-6

Unless indicated otherwise, all Scripture quotations in this publication are taken from the New King James Version (NKJV). Copyright © 1982 by Thomas Nelson, Inc. Used by permission. All rights reserved.

Scripture quotations marked (NIV) are from The Holy Bible, New International Version® (NIV®), copyright © 1973, 1978, 1984, 2011 by Biblica, Inc. ® Used by permission. All rights reserved worldwide. The "NIV" and "New International Version" are trademarks registered in the United States Patent and Trademark Office by Biblica, Inc.®

Scripture quotations marked (NLT) are taken from the Holy Bible, New Living Translation, copyright © 1996, 2004, 2015 by Tyndale House Foundation. Used by permission of Tyndale House Publishers, Inc., Carol Stream, Illinois 60188. All rights reserved.

Scripture quotations marked (MSG) are taken from The Message by Eugene Peterson. Copyright © 1993, 1994, 1995, 1996, 2000, 2001, 2002. Used by permission of NavPress Publishing Group. All rights reserved. Represented by Tyndale House Publishers, Inc.

Scripture quotations marked (KJV) are taken from the Holy Bible, King James Version. Public domain.

Cover Design: Josh Huffman
Interior Layout: Brett Burner
Editing: Nicole Terada

1 2 3 4 5 6 7 8 / 25 24 23

Introduction

Fame.

You may remember the musical that premiered in 1980 by this name. If you don't, ask your parents.

In pulling this off-Broadway play and movie from the recesses of my memory, I also pulled the lyrics back from the depths. The first two lines from the chorus are tragic. A complete lie, in the sense of what the composers must have meant.

Remember my name (Fame)
I'm gonna live forever

Seems as if everybody dreams about being rich and famous. But rarely does anyone discuss the price of fame. The fact is, fame has taken a heavy toll on countless men and women throughout the years. And ultimately, even if your name is remembered for a long time after you die, you *will* die . . . and your name will eventually die with you.

David Bowie had a pointed musical take on fame. "Fame puts you there where things are hollow," the Thin White Duke sang. "Fame, what you get is no tomorrow . . . Could it be the best, could it be?"

Maybe not, but deep down inside it's what so many people want.

The mansions. The adoration. The klieg lights. The limos. The boats. The jets. The islands. Designer clothes. Expensive cars. White glove treatment. Being able to get anything you want with a smile or nod. From where most people stand, it all looks great.

Andy Warhol once said, "In the future, everyone will be world-famous for fifteen minutes." Turns out, he was pretty close. In the age of social media, that concept has exploded.

It used to be that you had to have some kind of talent to become famous. You had to be a charismatic actor, a gifted athlete, or a talented musician. Now to get your fifteen minutes of fame, all you have to do is something outrageous to get attention. Talent, charisma, and ability are no longer any kind of determinants for fame. You can hold an American flag during a Florida hurricane. You can own a particularly ugly cat. You can stuff seventy-five hot dogs down your throat in ten minutes or less. Or you can have a catchy nickname on a reality show and land national endorsement deals in the millions.

Even Warhol couldn't have imagined this.

USA Today recently took a poll among young people. It revealed that more than anything an overwhelming majority of their generation wanted to become rich and famous—not to become a doctor or diplomat, or find a cure for cancer, or do something meaningful and productive. Only ten percent aspired to become more spiritual. Such is the pull of fame.

But people who are on the other side look at it differently.

Actor and comedian Jim Carrey said, "I think everybody should get rich and famous and do everything they ever dreamed of so they can see that it's not the answer."

Pop icon Justin Bieber felt the same way. A while back he posted an Instagram message that made many people take notice: "Hey World, that glamorous lifestyle you see portrayed by famous people on Instagram—Don't be fooled thinking their life is better than yours. I can promise you it's not."

Bieber made that post when he was twenty-seven years old. It comes from the heart of someone who became extremely famous at a young age, graduated from his wild teen years, and is now married and finding faith. Other stars that exact same age haven't fared so well.

Have you ever heard of the "27 Club"?

It's an informal list of stars who died at that age. We're talking Brian Jones, Jimi Hendrix, Janis Joplin, Jim Morrison, Amy Winehouse, and Kurt Cobain. The latter's mother, Wendy O'Connor, famously said after her son and the leader of Nirvana died, "Now he's gone and joined that stupid club."

Swedish DJ and electronic dance music (EDM) superstar Tim Bergling, better known as Avicii, made it to twenty-eight. He was at the top of his game, making millions of dollars, and had what most people dream of today: fame and money. According to his family, Avicii struggled with thoughts about meaning, life, and happiness.

"He could not go on any longer. He wanted to find peace," said his family in an open letter to fans and the media in 2018, the same year he committed suicide. "Tim was not made for the business machine he found himself in; he was a sensitive guy who loved his fans but shunned the spotlight."

Other well-known celebrities have taken their lives over the decades: Marilyn Monroe, Ernest Hemingway, Anthony Bourdain, Kate Spade, Hunter S. Thompson, Brad Delp, Keith Emerson, Margot Kidder, Dana Plato, Chris Cornell, Chester Bennington, Mindy McCready, Tony Scott, Alexander McQueen.

All of these people at one time or another had the world at their feet—and it wasn't fulfilling. If fame and money were the answers, why did so many make such a heartbreaking choice?

Can you relate?

Do you feel as if you can't go on any longer?

Do you want to find peace?

You're not alone.

Since the COVID-19 pandemic, many people are depressed and despondent. Counselors, therapists, psychologists, and pharmaceutical companies can hardly keep up with the demand. It's sad that this generation, who should be having the time of their lives, is anxious, depressed, and medicated.

Is there a way to deal with this hole in our hearts? The answer is yes, but not in the way you might think.

My wife, Cathe, likes puzzles. I have no idea why; I can walk right past them. The other day, she was completing a puzzle that she had been working on for hours downstairs in our house. Near the end, she called to me upstairs and said, "Greg, I finished the puzzle but I'm missing the final piece."

So I came downstairs and joined Cathe in the search. We got on our hands and knees, and I eventually found it. Life can be that way. We figure if we can just put the puzzle pieces in place, everything will be right: a good education, a family, a career, maybe a little religion. But something is missing.

Actually, some*one* is missing. And that someone is God.

Here are some more famous people who all have something in common. They all found success, fame, and something else . . . They found God.

Bono, Alice Cooper, Denzel Washington, Mel Gibson, Justin Bieber, Hailey Bieber, Russell Wilson, Ciara, Tyler Perry, Manny Pacquiao, Kathie Lee Gifford, Ruth Pointer, Paul Walker, Darryl Strawberry, Jeff Foxworthy, Mark Wahlberg, Larry the Cable Guy, Tim Tebow, Kathy Ireland, Jordin Sparks, Chris Pratt, Chuck Norris, Mr. Rogers, Carrie Underwood, and Johnny Cash.

Surprised at some of those names?

You might be.

Faith isn't something often discussed in Hollywood, a recording studio, or backstage at a concert.

But God made a difference in their lives, and He can make a difference in yours so that you can find the peace that has eluded so many.

Let's look closer at a few people who have found both fame and God, starting with the coolest star in cinematic history . . .

FAME

FORTUNES, FAILURE AND FAITH

ONE

TRADING FAME FOR FAITH

You may be too young to remember Steve McQueen, but I'm not. He was the highest paid movie star in the world in the 1960s and '70s, the ultimate alpha male of his generation. His tough-guy persona melded an unlikely combination of willfulness, unpredictability, strength, and vulnerability, which riveted audiences in such unforgettable films as *The Magnificent Seven*, *The Great Escape*, *The Thomas Crown Affair*, *Bullitt*, *The Getaway*, *Papillon*, and *The Towering Inferno*.

This real-life daredevil lived his life the way he drove his motorcycles and cars: fearlessly and at top speed.

But in December 1979, life slammed on the brakes when he was diagnosed with mesothelioma, a type of cancer caused from exposure to asbestos. He lived for another year and died just days after meeting Billy Graham. However, there's a part of his final years that many of the idolaters, wannabes, and steadfast keepers and stokers of McQueen's eternal flame conveniently ignore, deny, or dismiss as an aberration. It is, however, indisputable fact. Their rabble-rousing hero reached out to God to fill the void in his heart, to find the peace that consistently eluded him throughout his pedal-to-the-metal life.

Six months before receiving his cancer diagnosis, McQueen—in a seeming contradiction of his take-no-prisoners nature—quietly gave his life to the Lord on the balcony of an out-of-the-way church in Ventura, California. It wasn't a deathbed conversion.

What led him to such an unlikely decision—one that, on its face, seems so at odds with the Steve McQueen millions remember?

I had a personal reason for wanting to find out, and I told the story of the King of Cool's conversion in a 2017 book I wrote called *Steve McQueen: The Salvation of an American Icon*, as well as its companion documentary film.

The story is so good that it bears briefly repeating here.

Steve McQueen was born into the home of an alcoholic mother and a father who left him early in life. McQueen found himself on the wrong side of the law more than once. He chased after every pleasure this planet had to offer. His search led him through Hollywood, the best and fastest cars money could buy, multiple women, including two divorces, well-documented drug and alcohol abuse, and much more.

I have always admired McQueen as an actor and all around "guy's guy." Half a century ago, nobody embodied the notion of what a real man was, or made a bigger impression on adolescent males, than McQueen. He was a mainstay of my childhood and teen years.

McQueen successfully transitioned from a start in television to big-league movies, beginning with *Never So Few* (1959). A year later came *The Magnificent Seven*, in which his portrayal of one of the gunslingers hired to protect a besieged Mexican village stamped McQueen as a rising Hollywood star. In 1963, *The Great Escape* made him a one-star constellation, and he never had to worry about employment as an actor ever again. As the character Virgil Hilts, McQueen crafted one of the greatest screen personas, transcending the prototype of the strong and silent martyr.

McQueen owned the '60s and the first part of the '70s in terms of stardom, popularity, and the mountaintop we know as Hollywood. In those years, he chased after every worldly pleasure once he realized how fame widened his sphere of female admirers. That approach to life would surely bring its consequences, but he wouldn't know that until he discovered the love and forgiveness of Christ near the end of his life.

Even after God became the center of my life in 1970, Steve McQueen always intrigued me. Everything about him fascinated me: his hardscrabble beginnings, his meteoric rise to stardom, then his tragic end when cancer claimed him at age fifty.

McQueen's momentous conversion reportedly occurred just before the release of his last western film, *Tom Horn*. In fact, that's what drew me to the theater to see it, in addition to plain old curiosity. His last big hit, *The Towering Inferno*, co-starring Paul Newman, came out in December 1974, smashing all box-office records, and was then the highest grossing movie of all time. But then McQueen decided to take a break from filmmaking, and no one saw him on screen for about a five-year period.

When he finally reappeared in *Tom Horn*, McQueen looked as weather-beaten as an old saddle. It was hard to see such a symbol of youthful rebellion looking so old. In *The Hunter*, released on July 28, 1980, McQueen seemed even more spent. The wear and tear of hard living was evident on him. He appeared downright lethargic. I left the theater sad and disappointed.

Not quite three months later, Steve McQueen was dead.

Years later, I discovered that Billy Graham had paid McQueen a visit just days before his demise. The revelation came from a member of my church, a guy named Mike Jugan.

I told the story of Steve McQueen's unexpected conversion before a crowd of forty-five thousand people on a warm summer night in August 2016 at Angel Stadium in Anaheim for an event called the SoCal Harvest. People young and old were riveted by the story of a troubled boy who became the number-one movie star in the world, but turned to God after being disillusioned by the sheer emptiness of all he'd accumulated and accomplished. The message was well received and garnered over 100,000 views on YouTube.

A week later, Mike Jugan approached me after a service and asked if we could speak privately. Mike, a friend and terrific Christian, is a former pilot for Alaska Airlines. He also happened to be copilot of the airplane that had flown Steve McQueen to El Paso, Texas, in a last-ditch effort to save the actor's life.

I sat Mike down and urged him to tell me everything, and not to leave out a single detail. The story was absolutely stunning. And true.

Mike at the time was twenty-five, flying for Ken Haas Aviation, a Learjet charter company in Long Beach. On November 3, 1980, he went to the airport at Oxnard, California, to fly a party of three to El Paso. The group was registered under the name "Sam Sheppard," but that was an alias designed to throw off the paparazzi, who had been hounding McQueen ever since the *National Enquirer* months before broke a sensational story on McQueen's grave condition. Now the media was hounding him. Tabloid editors even put a bounty on his head: $50,000 for a photo of an ailing, cancer-ridden Steve McQueen.

Mike discovered the three passengers were actually Steve McQueen and two medical aides. He could barely believe it. McQueen had been his boyhood hero ever since he'd taken up motocross racing as a boy.

When Mike and Ken Haas got to the airport, they parked the jet far from the terminal in an effort to afford McQueen as much privacy as possible. As they sat in the cockpit waiting for their passengers to arrive, they heard a knock on the side of the plane.

"Are you with the Sam Sheppard party?" asked a tall man wearing an overcoat and hat. When Mike answered affirmatively, the man stuck out his hand and introduced himself.

"I'm Billy Graham," he said.

After the initial shock wore off, Billy told Mike and Ken that Steve McQueen and the others would be arriving shortly. After a few minutes, a pickup truck with a custom aluminum camper, where McQueen was lying down and receiving oxygen, pulled up. The truck wheeled under the canopy that had been set up over the forward part of the aircraft to shield McQueen from paparazzi or other curiosity seekers. Out of the truck stepped McQueen, sporting blue jeans, a T-shirt, and a sombrero, with a bottle of soda in his hand.

"Howdy, fellas," McQueen greeted the pilots.

"I'm standing there," recalled Mike, "looking at my childhood hero, and my heart went out to him. You could see his belly was distended and swollen from the tumors." But Mike also noticed something else:

> "The look in his crystal blue eyes was predictably fierce. He had this indomitable spirit about him, and he seemed to be at peace."

Accompanying McQueen were nurses Teena Valentino and Annie Martell. As the trio entered the plane, Billy gathered the folks around him and asked God to bless the pilots, the flight itself, and McQueen. Then before leaving, the famed evangelist stepped aboard for a final private word with the actor.

Mike told me that after the plane reached cruising altitude, he went back to chat with McQueen, and found him snacking on crackers and soda.

"I wanted to talk about motorcycles," said Mike, "but he was more interested in the plane and asked what it was like to fly a Learjet."

When they landed in El Paso, McQueen's party was whisked off to the clinic in Juarez, just across the Mexican border. McQueen had made arrangements for a doctor there to excise his cancerous tumors—a nontraditional approach that would only end up igniting other complications. That's why, four days later, on November 7, 1980, Mike and his boss were notified that McQueen had passed away and were asked to return in *two* jets this time: one for the actor's family, close friends, and medical staff; the other to carry McQueen's body back to California.

Mike piloted the jet that carried McQueen's casket, while Ken Haas flew the plane with McQueen's widow, Barbara; his two children, Chad and Terry; his caretaker Grady Ragsdale; his doctor Dwight McKee, and the other medical personnel who'd devoted months trying to save McQueen's life.

"Before boarding the flight, Barbara was crying," Mike recalled. "Terry and Chad were crying. The doctors and nurses were crying. It was very sad. I remember thinking to myself that just a few days before, Steve was so positive about the whole trip."

"I mean, this wasn't supposed to happen. He wasn't supposed to die."

As Mike was telling me all of this, his mention of Barbara McQueen made me wonder how she was doing now, and if he had any idea about that. It turned out that he and Barbara were friends, having met at a "Remembering Steve McQueen" event in 2008 in Santa Paula, California (where McQueen lived at the time of his death). Mike had read about the event in the newspaper, and the story mentioned that Barbara McQueen would be the guest of honor. So he decided to go and pay his respects.

He found Barbara and a mutual friend together at a Santa Paula hotel lobby and, upon being introduced to her, brought up that he was one of the pilots who had taken her husband to El Paso, that he'd flown the plane that had brought his body back to California.

> Mike told me he'd never forget the look of total shock on her face—how she then excused herself and ran into the ladies' room.

He felt terrible, afraid that he had single-handedly ruined what was supposed to be a weekend-long celebration for her and her late husband. But a few minutes later Barbara reemerged and said, "I have questions." They talked for a couple of hours about the two flights, as well as other matters related to McQueen's death. As they reached the end of their conversation, Barbara had slipped her hand in Mike's before saying goodbye, a quiet but powerful gesture of trust and kinship. They've stayed in touch ever since.

As Mike told me this, it occurred to me that if anyone would know how, if, and when Steve McQueen had given his life to the Lord, it would be the woman who was constantly at his side in his last years. Barbara McQueen was the answer to the mystery, and in my growing excitement, I asked Mike if he would be willing to arrange for me to meet and talk with her.

"I'll give it a try," he said. "All she can do is say no."

A meeting was arranged but Barbara initially refused. She said she didn't need some "preacher man" glomming onto a story to exploit it for his own purposes. I told Mike not to press the matter with Barbara. But God bless him, he didn't listen. He suggested she watch my sermon where I talked about Steve. She watched it, liked it, but especially liked the sneakers I wore that day. She said she'd meet with me, but it had to be on her terms.

"Okay," Barbara told Mike.

"Call the preacher man and tell him I'll meet with him. But it has to be on my turf. He'll need to come to Idaho."

I met Barbara in early November 2016 on an unseasonably warm day. I flew into Sun Valley, Idaho, a mountain retreat for the rich and famous.

She took me on a tour of the house, the likes of which I'd never seen before. In her living room sat a king-size bed and a dining table adorned with leather vests, cowboy hats, and Native American drums.

We ended up in "Barbi's" four-car garage, which she called her "girl cave." She floored me when she said,

> "Steve never talked to me about religion. One day he came home and said, 'We're going to church.'"

Barbi also mentioned that if I really wanted to know more about Steve's conversion to Christianity, the answer was back in my home state with a man named Leonard DeWitt.

DeWitt was the pastor of the Ventura Missionary Church in Ventura, California, when Steve McQueen began attending church in the spring of 1979. One day I made the two-hour drive to see DeWitt at Steve McQueen's old Santa Paula hangar, and he told me how the McQueens sat in the balcony of the church with Sammy and Wanda Mason almost every Sunday. Steve had hired Sammy, a former test pilot for Lockheed and a strong Christian, to teach him how to fly a Stearman biplane.

Over time their little group expanded as Steve brought along his son, Chad, whenever he visited.

> Church became part of the weekly routine, and Steve McQueen began to change before people's eyes.

The change was a result of the time he spent with Sammy Mason. But the vintage Stearman wasn't the only thing McQueen was learning about from his hours in the air, because Sammy turned out to be much more than a flight instructor.

Sammy exuded confidence without braggadocio and drew the respect of everyone who knew him. Steve, too, was in awe of him. And as they became closer over the months, Steve started asking questions of his new mentor. What he wanted most to know was what gave Sammy the kind of serenity and peace that Steve had vainly searched for his entire life.

The answer, Sammy told him, was that he was a Christian.

Over time, they began to talk about God. Mason didn't preach or even try to persuade. The impenetrable armor Steve had developed over a lifetime was beginning to crack. He'd personally seen the emptiness of the life he lived, and he wanted to know more about the Christian walk.

There could not have been a better person to embrace Steve than Sammy, and eventually Steve and Barbi ended up alongside Sammy and his wife, Wanda, in the balcony of the Ventura Missionary Church for Sunday services.

The McQueens had attended services for about three months when Steve introduced himself to Pastor DeWitt.

McQueen invited him out to lunch, just the two of them. It was immediately apparent to Barbi that his session with DeWitt had had a profound effect on her husband.

"He was a little more quiet and reserved than usual," she recalled to me. "He seemed different."

DeWitt told me that McQueen had peppered him with questions about Christianity for the entire two-hour lunch.

"Steve wanted to know if all of his sins could be forgiven, if the Bible could be trusted, and what it looked like to be a Christian," DeWitt recounted.

DeWitt said he answered each of McQueen's questions as best as he could and recalls it as an intense conversation more than an interrogation. "Finally, Steve sat back, smiled, and said, 'Well, that about covers it for me,'" DeWitt recalled. Then DeWitt said he had only one question for Steve, but before he could ask it, Steve said, "You want to know if I'm a born-again Christian, right?"

DeWitt nodded and said, "Steve, that's all that's really important to me."

McQueen quietly revealed that during a service a few Sundays prior when the pastor invited everyone to pray with him to receive Christ, he had prayed and it had happened.

"Yes," said Steve. "I'm a born-again Christian."

Contrary to what some have written and said over the years about McQueen's profession of faith, it was not occasioned by the death sentence he received from doctors. Steve's meeting with DeWitt occurred fully six months before McQueen was diagnosed with cancer.

His decision to accept Christ was entirely of his own free will and totally unfettered by the specter of his final judgment day.

Sadly, in December 1979, DeWitt received a phone call from McQueen asking if they could meet. He knew by the tone of McQueen's voice "something major was going on." When they connected later that day, McQueen told DeWitt he had just been diagnosed with cancer.

"He said, 'Leonard, now that I know Christ, I really want to live. I believe God could use me, but if He doesn't heal me, it's okay because I know where I'm going,'" DeWitt recalled. "It was so transparent, so genuine, so honest."

McQueen's prognosis was grim, and a year later his cancer was out of control.

It had spread to the lining of his stomach, and tumors as big as golf balls were growing at the base of his neck and chest and abdomen. Surgery and chemotherapy would be futile, the doctors said. After spending time at a Mexican cancer clinic for last-ditch unorthodox treatments, he returned to his Santa Paula home in early November 1980. McQueen knew he was facing his end days and time was short.

Billy Graham had been made aware of McQueen's illness through DeWitt. Steve had mentioned in passing how much it would mean for him to meet Billy, and as McQueen's condition worsened, DeWitt picked up the phone.

"I made at least two phone calls," said DeWitt, who had a connection to Billy through his church. "The second time was to say that if Dr. Graham was going to come, it should be sooner rather than later."

Billy and Steve finally met on November 3, 1980, at McQueen's home in Santa Paula. Billy most likely knew that he was meeting the superstar on his deathbed, and that's not an easy task for any man of God. Though Billy had plenty of experience talking to people whose lives were about to expire (most notably former President Dwight D. Eisenhower), the task is never easy.

It turned out to be a momentous occasion for both men.

"He told me of his spiritual experience," Billy recalled later. "He said that about three months before he knew he was ill, he had accepted Christ as his Savior and had started going to church, reading his Bible, and praying. He said he had undergone a total transformation of his thinking and life."

McQueen told Billy how Sammy Mason had led him to the Lord and said it was his faith in Christ that helped him deal with his illness. Billy read several passages of Scripture, and they prayed together.

Billy then accompanied McQueen to the nearby Oxnard Airport, while Steve asked him questions about the afterlife. In the small private plane, they said a final prayer together. When Billy got up to go, he instinctively handed his personal Bible to McQueen. On the front inside flap he had written:

To my friend Steve McQueen. May God bless you and keep you always.
Billy Graham
Philippians 1:6
Nov. 3, 1980

Just before Billy exited the plane, Steve called out, "I'll see you in Heaven!"

Steve McQueen didn't survive the operation in Juarez, Mexico, suffering through two heart attacks after his surgery. He was pronounced dead at 3:54 on the morning of November 7. His nurse Teena Valentino was there, and his son Chad asked for his dad's watch and cowboy hat. He noticed that his father's eyes were open, looking blue as ever.

Steve McQueen had made the ultimate "Great Escape."

One other thing:

The Bible given to Steve by Billy—his most prized possession—was tightly clutched in Steve's hands on his deathbed.

Billy later explained what that visit to Steve McQueen ultimately meant to him. "I look back on that experience with thanksgiving and some amazement," Dr. Graham mused.

"I had planned to minister to Steve, but as a matter of fact, he had ministered to me."

"His cheerfulness, his bright eyes, his excitement about his relationship with God will never be forgotten. I saw once again the reality of what Jesus Christ can do for a man in his last hours."

Jesus was knocking on Steve McQueen's door throughout the years. And finally, when McQueen had come to the "end of himself," he came to the beginning of God, and he believed.

TWO

A BRIEF HISTORY OF FAME

Outracing Nazi troops on a motorcycle. Busting through burning doors in a flaming high rise. Chasing down mafia assassins in a Ford Mustang. Facing down rustlers alone.

That was Steve McQueen on screen. Off screen he was equally cool and charismatic. He was the consummate hero.

Ancient Greeks had a word for this: they called it *kleos*. It roughly translates to "renown" or "glory." Implied is "what others hear about you."

A Greek hero earned his *kleos* through performing great deeds.

That was the precursor to modern fame. Fame is being well known and in the public eye. Celebrity is a little different. There's less achievement involved but there's still recognition—good or bad. There are many celebrities today who are famous for just being famous. I don't have to list them. You know who they are. They appear on tabloid journalism sites like TMZ. They show up at nightclub openings. They guest DJ at the hottest spots and festivals. They have reality shows that make for mindless but mesmerizing entertainment. They appear on Instagram and make bank on a single post. They have huge followings on YouTube that follow their every move.

All of this is a modern phenomenon.

Were there "famous" people in history? Yes and no. Going back to the ancient world, there were "renowned" gladiators. Note, I did not use the word *famous*. These gladiators rarely lived past thirty. The number of gladiators who died peacefully in their sleep is probably in the single digits. Women may have been attracted to them, especially noble ones, but as far as fame goes, it's highly doubtful any Thracian fourteen-year-old girl had a mosaic of a gladiator with his trident on her bedroom wall. Plus, it wasn't like modern athletics. Between recovering from wounds and whatnot, a gladiator typically fought three times a year. Not exactly Tom Brady.

Julius Caesar was famous in the way that we think of it now, but he was also a ruler and a famous general. There was no mass media to hype his fame. However, his face was on every coin, and statues of him stood everywhere in Rome. His fame was amplified when he returned from successful campaigns, dragging captives behind his chariots in state-sponsored parades called "triumphs." Modern politicians only wish they could make an entrance like that.

How about Jesus? Was He famous? In His lifetime, that would be doubtful.

He likely was not very well known outside of the Holy Land, which at the time was a backwater Roman province. Certainly, He did things that got everyone's attention, but His exploits weren't publicized at the time or even written down until long after His death.

Some experts believe early twelfth-century English martyr Thomas Becket was the first famous person in the modern sense. After he was assassinated in Canterbury Cathedral, images of him in scenes from his life became widespread. People made pilgrimages to the site of his death and his life inspired plays in the aftermath of his passing.

Skipping ahead a few centuries, the first American celebrity was undoubtedly George Washington. Engravings, paintings, statues, and drawings of him were in many homes. He drew crowds wherever he went.

Keep in mind that democracy was completely new. No one was sure how to run it. It wasn't like European royalty with centuries of tradition and protocol. Because the country was run by the people, it was felt the people had a right to meet their leader.

So many people appeared at Washington's office to see him, he couldn't get anything done.

But his aides couldn't turn them away. So, they came up with an idea. For a few hours one day a week, anyone could show up, walk in, and meet the nation's first president. Washington hated it. He stiffly stood in full dress uniform by a fireplace greeting these well-intentioned intruders.

As with retired Hollywood stars, fanfare didn't end after Washington left office. He traveled around the country. At every town he entered, throngs turned out to cheer him, and dignitaries feted him with banquets and speeches. He may have even kissed a baby or two.

Long before the Beatles invaded America, Benjamin Franklin took Europe by storm as a part of the Revolutionary War. Franklin was an inventor, scientist, writer, and diplomat for our nation. The French welcomed Franklin with open arms, and he became a pop culture icon. Images of Franklin wearing a fur cap were seen in paintings, engravings, medallions, rings, snuffboxes, and hats.

A few decades after Washington stepped down from being Commander in Chief, another megastar in the modern mold appeared. Horatio Nelson is one of England's most famous sons, up there with Winston Churchill and Queen Elizabeth II. Nelson was a naval hero during the Napoleonic wars. His heroic derring-do was splashed across every newspaper every time he won another battle. His face stared out from prints, paintings, dishes, cups, statuettes, and every other kind of tacky junk you can imagine. Trafalgar Square in London is named after his most famous victory, and a life-size statue of him looks down on traffic jams and throngs of pedestrians.

Back on the other side of the pond, more than half a century later, the American frontier was bustling with characters, not a few of whom weren't shy about self-promotion. Among them were Buffalo Bill, Billy the Kid, Doc Holliday, and "Wild Bill" Hickok, who became famous a second time when he traded in his pistol for grease paint. The frontiersman was not a triumph on the stage. His delivery was flat, he often hid behind scenery, and he once shot out a spotlight when it was trained on him. The crowd loved it though.

The gunfighters were aware of their reputations and were not above writing angry letters to newspapers about their portrayal when they felt it was inaccurate or unflattering. They were usually along the lines of "I shot six men, not two" or "I was nowhere near that stagecoach when it was robbed."

Geronimo, the famous Apache warrior, found an easy income after his surrender. He sold autographs, postcards, and photos of himself to enthusiastic crowds at world fairs and other large gatherings. It wasn't cheap, either. He earned up to $2 a day. Today one of his penciled autographs can fetch up to $20,000, a lot more than a signed photo of Carrot Top.

But Geronimo didn't live into the age of Hollywood, which created a world where there were scores of famous celebrities instead of just a few. Among the early Hollywood famous were Buster Keaton, Mae West, Tom Mix, Clara Bow, "Fatty" Arbuckle, Mary Pickford, Rudolph Valentino, Lillian Gish, Gloria Swanson, Marion Davies, and William S. Hart.

None of these approached the stardom of Charlie Chaplin, however. The comic actor, filmmaker, and composer was internationally famous, largely through his screen persona, the Tramp. He brought the term "movie star" into the popular lexicon. His unique brand of slapstick gave audiences much-needed comic relief through the Great Depression and the two World Wars. His was one of the first known instances where fame had a double edge. The tabloids took notice of his penchant for young women, one of whom filed a paternity suit against him. The case was ultimately dismissed because it was proven the child in question was not biologically his. Since then, however, scandal has become a mainstay of standard Hollywood publicity.

Fame has become a huge part of American cultural life, and its dark side is darker than ever.

Steve McQueen and Rock Hudson were hunted down on their deathbeds by paparazzi. Reporters snapped photos of Elvis Presley in his casket and John Lennon in the morgue. Media outlets would gleefully run pictures of celebrities who were without makeup, drunk in public, or in any number of unflattering situations.

And that was forty years ago. Now the intensity has been dialed up by the twenty-four-seven news cycle, celebrity journalism, gossip blogs, and social media. The celebrities of yesteryear had it easy compared to the microscope today's stars live under.

Imagine being Leonardo DiCaprio, Tom Cruise, Lady Gaga, or Angelina Jolie. Simply put, these people cannot have normal lives.

They can't walk into an airport or grocery store without being mobbed. DiCaprio was recently asked by a reporter the moment that he knew he was famous. He replied it was in the days after the movie *Titanic* premiered. He said when he went on an outing to a convenience store to pick up a pack of smokes, the paparazzi was there in full force, snapping his photo and shouting his name.

"I knew then my life would never be the same again," DiCaprio said.

I've already mentioned that the majority of today's young people want to become rich and famous. Let's be honest. The mansions, the cars, the wealth, and the adoration have a lot of allure for many of us—not just the kids. But that's because we don't know what it's really like to wear the fame suit.

In this book, you're going to hear what it's like on the other side of the velvet rope. Forget any kind of privacy. There are numerous stories from celebrities about being hounded for autographs, even in a bathroom stall. Famous people endure plenty of outlandish behavior and requests, and they are often poked and prodded like they're part of a petting zoo. Every bad thing they'd ever done in their life gets resurrected by the press; any off-color joke they might have made is revived and dissected. Their tweets, college antics, and youthful indiscretions are dragged into glaring daylight for all to see.

American icon Johnny Cash succinctly summarized fame this way: "Public life is unbelievable . . . Being a 'star' means so many things and all of them opposite of normalcy. If your face is familiar, you are stared at, pointed at, laughed at, whispered at, yelled at, and followed.

"People say lots of things about you that they wouldn't say if they knew you heard.

"Everything you do well is taken for granted. Any mistake is a matter for great attention."

Cash was speaking from a place of experience. He was famous for almost half a century, and his fame colored and complicated his life to the very end. Let's examine this in the next chapter.

THREE

FROM MAN IN BLACK TO MAN IN WHITE

Johnny Cash was many things in his seventy-one turbulent years on Earth: a country music artist who sang and acted in a rock and roll context; a social activist and a jailbird; an evangelist and an addict; a humanitarian who disdained and often butted heads with authority figures; a husband and an adulterer; a master storyteller and a world-class embellisher; an outlaw with the soul of a mystic; and an impossible, tortured man who pinballed back and forth between extremes.

Cash was constantly in the news. Not all the headlines were admirable. He was often embroiled in scandal or controversy stemming from high-profile arrests, car accidents, and other drug and alcohol-induced escapades, including one resulting in a forest fire that devastated 508 acres. His music and social activism gave light and hope to others, but Cash's dark side often overruled his true nature.

"I confess right up front that I'm the biggest sinner of them all," Cash said once.

"But my faith in God has always been a solid rock that I've stood on, no matter where I was or what I was doing. I was a bad boy at times, but God was always there for me, and I knew that. I guess maybe I took advantage of that."

Maybe?

He never killed anyone, but the other nine of God's Commandments were fair game for the "Man in Black." Cash's enormous successes were rivaled by a litany of personal tribulations.

He was a walking, talking contradiction who identified with the apostle Peter (often ashamed and lacking the courage to stand up for Christ) in the first half of his life. All of these traits and foibles were rolled up into a larger-than-life, one-of-a-kind personality that put its unique, indelible stamp on pop music and culture.

Cash was a knowledgeable Christian who divided his time between sinning and seeking forgiveness, often going from jail to Jesus.

He was arrested five times in one seven-year span. He knew almost every hymn and gospel tune ever sung, often performing them in shows between hit songs like "I Walk the Line," "Ring of Fire," and "Cocaine Blues." He saw God as the Number One power in the world but viewed Satan as a close second.

"I learned not to laugh at the Devil," Cash was once famously quoted.

Cash was introduced to Jesus Christ as a dirt-poor child in the midst of the Great Depression. On his twelfth birthday, Cash attended a revival meeting and went forward as the congregation sang the hymn "Just as I Am." But his new faith was shaken to its core when he lost his older brother Jack in a gruesome accident. Johnny described Jack as "my hero, my best friend, my big buddy, and my mentor." Johnny claimed he was visited by an angel, a man dressed in a gray suit. Johnny asked the man if he could take Jack's place. "No," said the angel with an emphatic shake of his head, "it's not your time."

The Man in Black was a touchstone in my life dating back to my childhood, which is why I penned a book and produced a documentary about him titled, *Johnny Cash: The Redemption of an American Icon*.[1] I remember watching him with my grandparents as he performed on television and hearing that deep booming voice, once called "The Voice of America." An even more indelible memory is of my grandfather, who read

---

1   Greg Laurie, *Johnny Cash: The Redemption of an America Icon* (Salem Books, 2019).
Johnny Cash: The Redemption of an America Icon (film), Directed by Ben Smallbone, (Kingdom Story Company and Harvest Ministries, 2022).

the newspaper religiously, coming across a mention of one of Cash's frequent brushes with the law. When that happened, my grandfather, whom we called "Daddy Charles," gave the paper a quick shake, shot my grandmother a disapproving look, and said to her,

"Well, your cousin's in trouble again." *Whoa— were we related to Johnny Cash?*

A man named Nettie Cash Fowler was a relative on my grandmother's side. I know nothing about him, but we have an "Old West"-style photo of him in my family album. He has a distant look on his face, and his arms are crossed. There's a gun in one hand and a large knife in the other. He looked like trouble.

Fowler was my grandmother Stella's last name when she married Charles McDaniel. So, even if she were only a distant relative of the famed entertainer, Daddy Charles never let her forget it.

The possibility isn't that far-fetched. Johnny Cash was born in Kingsland, Arkansas, and my grandparents hailed from Friendship, Arkansas, about an hour's drive away. When they moved to Southern California in the 1930s, they brought their Southern Baptist values and work ethic with them. They were like parents to me when I was sent to live with them while their daughter Charlene—my mother—was living her wild life.

During the time I was with them, it was almost like I was being raised in another century. Among the old-fashioned values they instilled in me was showing respect for and obedience to your elders . . . or else! More than once, Daddy Charles applied the "board of education" to my "seat of understanding."

I absorbed those values as thoroughly as I lapped up the tasty Southern dishes my grandmother prepared: fried chicken, mashed potatoes, black-eyed peas, okra, cornbread, and her crowning achievement: buttermilk biscuits made from scratch.

> Johnny Cash also lived in two worlds—one in fame and one in faith. The result was paradoxical. He was both a sinner and a saint.

To many sinners, he was a saint, even a prophet-like figure. Cash was admired by idols of days gone by ranging from Elvis Presley, Paul McCartney, and Carl Perkins to modern-day rockers like Bono, Sheryl Crow, Jack White, and Trent Reznor.

To many saints, he was a conflicted man, struggling with drugs and the law and a lot more that most people don't know about.

> In reality, John R. Cash was a lot like you and a lot like me.

And yet, he was completely unique as well. Who else could be friends with Willie Nelson, Bono, and Billy Graham at the same time? Who else could play a large Las Vegas showroom and a Billy Graham Crusade in the same week? Who else could play a gospel tune to a roomful of murderers, rapists, and thieves and have them eating out of the palm of his hand?

It's often said that it's best not to meet the people you admire most because you'll end up wishing you hadn't, but I doubt that would've been the case with Johnny Cash.

The closest I ever got to him was in Portland, Oregon. I was there assisting Billy Graham with one of his crusades. I was just beginning my evangelistic ministry then, and Billy's was slowly coming to a close. Johnny and his wife June Carter Cash sang that night, and at intervals, I staked out the stage area during soundcheck, as well as their dressing room, but I never even got within shouting distance of him. I should've tried harder.

Like millions of people, I was touched personally by Cash's life and music. When I became a Christian in 1970, the "Jesus Revolution," as *Time* magazine dubbed it, was in full swing. The high-water mark for many of us was a massive event called Explo '72 in Dallas, Texas, that brought new forms of worship into the church and paved the way for contemporary Christian music. Adding star-studded legitimacy was the presence of Billy Graham and a host of performers such as Kris Kristofferson, Love Song, Andraé Crouch and the Disciples . . . and Johnny Cash.

Having the famous and infamous Johnny Cash identify as "one of us" was a big deal.

No disrespect intended, but Ernest Tubb just wouldn't have cut it.

In addition to being "the Man in Black," Johnny Cash was also "the Godfather of Cool." To me, being cool is to be real and authentic. It's not the person who morphs with the latest trends; it's the person who stays true to who he is. It's authenticity. It's being real—and original.

Johnny Cash was an American icon, though he never copped to that.

"I see the pimples on my nose and I see a fat jaw where the pain has left me severely swollen, thinning hair, whatever," Cash said to an interviewer. "Icon? No, I don't see him. He's not in my mirror . . . No, thanks anyway."

But Cash was that icon—and he was also an unashamed follower of Jesus Christ.

When your fame is stratospheric like his was, it doesn't always mesh well with your faith. He acted humble, but like most celebrities and famous people, he had an ego that needed constant stroking. It's so hard to get to the top that most people are never certain they've really arrived. They need to hear that, yes, they are in fact a star.

There were struggles and inconsistencies and addiction, different shades of darkness, and varying depths of sadness that came with his chronic abuse of drugs. He seemed to be swimming in different directions at all times, and too often he was barely treading water.

In the throes of his addiction to amphetamines, he started hearing voices—demons.

Once, sitting in his camper in the middle of the night, stewed to the gills on Dexedrine, he put his hand over his face and peeped through his fingers at his reflection in the rearview mirror.

"Let's kill us," the demons urged.

"I *can't* be killed," Cash told his reflection. "I'm indestructible."

"I dare you to try."

So Cash started up the camper and headed down the side of a steep mountain. The vehicle rolled over twice, and Cash broke his jaw in two places. But he'd showed those demons all right. He was indestructible.

Later, he didn't want to be indestructible anymore.

His twelve-year marriage to a loving, dutiful wife named Vivian had crumbled, and he had left four daughters in his wake of self-ruin. He had financial problems, and his credibility with concert promoters was shot. Thanks to a diet consisting mostly of amphetamines, he had wasted away to a gaunt 150 pounds—almost skeletal for his six-foot-two frame. And when the tremors caused by the pills had him climbing the walls, he switched to barbiturates to calm himself down. He gulped down lots of beer in between.

But Cash always went back to what was true, and he had a knack for turning his suffering around. It usually started with repenting and returning to the spiritual well.

When he married singer June Carter a few years later, the couple answered an altar call by a preacher who summoned the congregation to "get off the fence with your faith." John and June rededicated their lives to the Lord in a small Assemblies of God church in Nashville, and the longtime prodigal returned.

But every day was still a struggle. "I fight the beast in me every day," Cash said. "I've won a few rounds with God's help."

The 1970s and 1980s were filled with peaks and valleys, career ups and downs and yo-yoing addiction. The cancellation of *The Johnny Cash Show* in 1971 marked the end of an era in many ways. It was his most fruitful professional period, the apex of his global fame, and the time of his most prodigious and commercial output as an artist.

Most importantly, it was also the true beginning of his spiritual life, engendered by a genuine desire to seek God and get right with Him.

To be sure, by then Cash was an old hand at petitioning God and hailing Him as the author of his salvation. But the fact is that he usually ran to God when a crisis was at hand and he needed rescuing, the same as you and me as mere mortals. Also, like some, Johnny was a natural backslider who kept God's number on speed-dial for emergencies. Sometimes he forgot to even call, especially when his addictions flared up. That usually happened when his career suffered a downturn like it did in the late 1970s. By then he had become a caricature of himself. Contemporaries like Kenny Rogers, Dolly Parton, Merle Haggard, and Glen Campbell were far outselling him. The Outlaw movement had kicked in, led by Waylon Jennings, Willie Nelson, Jessi Colter, and Tompall Glaser. Cash seemed as if he were out in the cold on his own, and he sought refuge once again in a pill bottle and relapsed in late 1977.

The 1980s weren't kind to Cash.

That decade was filled with setbacks, mishaps, and misadventures that surely would have killed a lesser man. Cash experienced a precipitous drop in popularity, a fight to stay relevant, lukewarm record sales, a worsening drug problem, marital woes, a robbery at gunpoint, financial problems, and health scares that nearly took him out.

His children finally staged an intervention and convinced the entertainer to check into the Betty Ford Center in Rancho Mirage, California, to get help.

After a forty-three-day stint at the facility, Cash came to the realization that drugs kept him separated from his Creator and his spiritual life.

He would need his faith to get him through the stormiest part of his career because no one was buying Johnny Cash's music.

By the mid-1980s, the good old boy network on Music Row had dramatically changed. The colorful mavericks and iconoclasts who took chances and reaped big rewards died off or retired, and their record companies were taken over by big media conglomerates. Once run by people who loved the music business, the labels were now in the clutches of buttoned-up bean counters who were "risk averse"; they disdained originality and avoided sticking their necks out. The aging Cash was not selling the numbers he used to, and

Columbia (the record label that Cash helped to build) kicked him to the curb in July 1986, after three decades.

He learned that he was dropped through a newspaper article.

The sacking had impacted Cash greatly. He was in shock, especially at the lack of respect afforded him. He was a respected artist but an irrelevant figure. It turned out to be the least of his worries. Six months after his release from Betty Ford, Cash was back on pills, though nowhere near his former abuse level. He did, however, check into another drug treatment center in Tennessee to prevent relapse. He cycled throughout the rest of his life this way.

With his recording career at its lowest ebb, Cash had to let some employees go, reduce the size of his band, and impose salary cuts on the musicians who stayed. He also sold his publishing catalog for some quick green. Johnny and June were even reduced to hocking jewelry to pay their large domestic staff.

The idea of playing Branson, Missouri, had once turned Cash's stomach. He, like many others, thought of it as a budget-class resort town and the last stand for creaking stars of yesteryear. But now that his fortunes and circumstances had dramatically changed (Cash hadn't had a bona fide country hit in a decade), Branson didn't seem so bad.

On a good night, half of the theater's three thousand seats were filled. Sometimes fewer than three hundred people turned out for a show. It was a far cry from the time he sold out Madison Square Garden.

But a wonderful thing happened to Johnny Cash when his ego was stripped away over time; it was the necessary evil to bring him to the end of himself.

His painful trials and tribulations led him through the valley of the shadow of death. His torrid past was naught either, because he used it to keep others from making the same mistakes he had. He dedicated the final decade of his life to sharing the knowledge that life apart from Christ was as useless as his vanity because it got him nowhere and led to an unfulfilled life.

For most of his adult life, Cash thought he was ten feet tall and bulletproof, but his health scares, the deaths of his parents, his financial woes, and his career nosedive showed him that the things of this world are not important compared to all eternity. In his more vulnerable state, he realized he was no longer indestructible, and it was God who was in charge, not Johnny Cash. He flourished when he allowed God to take over.

The final decade of Cash's life saw his fame and reputation on the ascent once more. Because of his partnership with Def Jam Records cofounder and producer Rick Rubin, almost overnight Cash went from Nashville has-been to hip icon in 1994. Their collaboration on the *American Recordings* sessions brought on loud, sustained hosannas from the critics and buying public alike. The new stripped-down sound was viscerally intimate, both intense and ambitious—its subjects touching on God, murder, salvation, forgiveness, and, of course, trains. It was a major artistic breakthrough, a vivid acoustic collection that stunned the music world and reintroduced a mythic American artist to rock audiences.

The MTV generation discovered Cash, and younger artists like U2, Tom Petty, Elvis Costello, Nine Inch Nails, Depeche Mode, and Kid Rock all paid homage in one form or another. The sixty-something Cash was relevant again.

College students and a new generation of metal heads, alt-rockers, punks, and goths now had a frenzied interest in the Godfather of Cool.

They saw in him a resilient, larger-than-life figure who had been through the wars and come out alive; a flawed hero who never complained or explained; an old warrior who didn't look back in anger or regret but only ahead to what tomorrow might bring; a towering, spellbinding American original.

Cash also entered a tranquil period of knee-bending Christianity as he faced his own mortality.

By the time he turned seventy, the ravages of time had caught up with him. He appeared frail and his thinning white hair made him look twenty years older. Diabetes and other ailments stripped him of his looks, his strength, and his sight.

The cruelest blow of all was the death of his wife, June Carter Cash, on May 15, 2003, as she was undergoing heart valve replacement surgery. Cash knew he wasn't far behind. He told journalist Kurt Loder in what turned out to be his last television interview, "I expect my life to end pretty soon. I'm seventy-one years old, but I have great faith. I have unshakable faith. I've never been angry with God. I've never turned my back on God. I've never thought God wasn't there. He's my counselor. He's my wisdom. All of the good things in my life come from Him."[2] And, less than five months after June's death, on September 12, Johnny Cash succumbed to respiratory failure due to complications from his long battle with diabetes.

He told everyone close to him that he could hardly wait to be with the Lord.

---

2   https://www.youtube.com/watch?v=i1zRFnw4jOU

Johnny Cash was a flawed individual, just like you and me. He sinned, and he was the first to admit it. But he knew where to turn to when he was in need, which was often.

He started and finished well, both musically and spiritually. He stands as a textbook example of a man who found that by His grace, God gives second chances in life, and he took full advantage of that again and again.

If Johnny Cash were here with us today, he would want us to know that eternity is real, and God's promises are trustworthy.

I am confident, based on his life and words and songs, that he would want you to find the same peace and satisfaction in a relationship with God through Jesus Christ that he had.

On his deathbed, fame isn't what Johnny Cash wanted or reached for. It was the hand of Jesus.

FOUR

NOTHING NEW UNDER THE SUN

You might be surprised to learn that many famous creative people come from hardscrabble backgrounds and upbringings. This creates a drive in them to overcome, to get even, to prevail, to not be put down any longer. It's hard to hold them back. Their talent becomes their escape— the only thing that gives them relief and quells the nagging insecurity. They find their new place, whether that be a baseball diamond, a recording studio, a Hollywood backlot, or a red-carpet appearance.

Steve McQueen grew up migrating from relative to relative and attended reform school. Marilyn Monroe's mother was diagnosed as a paranoid schizophrenic and was literally dragged away to a mental hospital, so the screen legend grew up in an orphanage and was raised by foster parents. Johnny Cash grew up dirt poor in rural Arkansas and picked cotton for most of his young life. Actress Halle Berry lived in a homeless shelter in New York City shortly after her twenty-first birthday. Janis Joplin was bullied by her Port Arthur, Texas, high school classmates, who called her a pig and threw pennies at her for running with the beatnik crowd.

These types of experiences scarred their souls but, in a way, prepared all of these celebrities to scale the heights because they had learned to build a resilience to rejection.

What they could not anticipate or prepare for was what came next: Fame.

When fame arrives, it comes out of nowhere at a speed no one expects. At first, when careers are launched, it feels like everything takes forever and you're getting nowhere. There's a lot of downtime, endless rejection, and feeling low. But when it finally hits, you feel you've created something bigger than you expected; sometimes you can't keep up with it. The new you might not fit like a glove, but a series of adjustments are usually made to adapt. Overnight, the doubt goes away and you are the king of the mountain. Very few are ready for the ride to Candyland.

That's when the partying begins.

You're on TMZ every day. Your every move is featured on Page Six in the *New York Post*. Your picture even gets taken when you're walking the dog in sweats, usually unshaven or with no makeup. You know you've really made it when the paparazzi show up to wherever you are and your publicist didn't even tip them off.

And when you get to that level of stardom, whom are you going to listen to?

Who is going to tell you what to do? Your ego goes haywire because one minute you're a smalltown country kid and the next thing you know, a hero of your youth is in your green room or VIP area and is telling you how much he or she admires you.

You're not going to listen to the school of fish that now seems to accompany you everywhere: the publicist, the hairstylist, the wardrobe assistant, the bodyguard, the manager, the accountant, the agent, or the personal assistant. Your parents can't even tell you what to do, because even after you've bought them the house, the car, first-class airfare, and all the rest . . . they have no idea what this is like.

Essentially, you're not a person anymore.

You are not entitled to the privacy or the peace normal people get. You don't get to be too tired or not in the mood to smile for a photo, sign an autograph, thank them for being a fan, or listen to what they think about your last game, movie, or single.

I've seen this up close many times. I can tell you from experience, many of these stars find it exhausting to be "on" all the time, to have a smile welded to their faces for hours on end. It's draining to not be able to say what you're really thinking for fear it might end up in *The National Enquirer*, in a venomous tweet, or as a talking point on *The View*.

Actress Justine Bateman calls it "performing your role" all the time. If you recall, Bateman was a star in a hit sitcom in the 1980s called *Family Ties*. She played Mallory, a material girl who was essentially interested in two things: shopping and boys. Bateman, a smoker at the time, was in a bar smoking a cigarette and talking to her friend. A stranger approached her, interrupted the conversation, and said, "Mallory doesn't smoke." This person, a stranger, let it be known he was disappointed. That goodwill toward Bateman's role was trashed.

When you are forced to constantly perform your role, "you forget to behave in any other way," Bateman said.

You are no longer yourself. You start doing things you think other people will like.

Robert Relyea, one of Steve McQueen's closest business associates, once said of the movie star, "Steve has the greatest need to be liked of anyone I know."

The Romans had a god named Janus. He represented doors, gates, and transitions. Janus had four faces. I get the feeling Janus would have done well in Hollywood, a place, as Marilyn Monroe noted, "where they'll pay you a thousand dollars for a kiss and fifty cents for your soul."

In time, celebrities know their fame has nothing to do with reality. But after they've had a taste of it, they want more of it. One of the worst side effects is believing your own press releases and acting terribly behind the scenes. As podcaster Joe Rogan recently said, "If you have this smooth sailing life where you put your hand outside the shower and someone hands you a towel, it's not healthy."

Another comedian, John Mulaney, once wrote for *Saturday Night Live*. Mick Jagger was the guest host. He came to Mulaney's cramped office to work on a comedic bit for the show. Jagger plopped down on the couch, stretched out his hand, and barked, "DIET COKE!" A Diet Coke was immediately thrust in Sir Mick's palm by one of his fast-acting handlers. Fifty years on a stage with millions of people screaming at you like you're a god has to change a person, Mulaney remarked.

Modern day celebrities had nothing on King Solomon. He had seven hundred wives and limitless wealth. His reign started off well, but then he began to squander his opportunities in pursuit of pure hedonism. There were epic drinking binges and many parties. He had a thousand women at his beck and call, many of whom were his personal concubines. He would have embarrassed Motley Crüe on a Saturday night at the LA Forum in their prime.

When he eventually took stock of his life, Solomon wrote: "I took a good look at everything I'd done, looked at all the sweat and hard work. But when I looked, I saw nothing but smoke. Smoke and spitting into the wind. There was nothing to any of it. Nothing" (Ecclesiastes 2:11 MSG).

Twenty-one hundred years later, does any of this sound familiar?

> People chase after the same empty things, generation after generation, ignoring what Solomon learned: "There is nothing new under the sun" (Ecclesiastes 1:9 NKJV).

History is a great teacher. If you study it closely, you realize nothing new ever happens. Sadly, few people learn anything from history and are doomed to repeat the same mistakes. That especially rings true when it comes to fame. Yet more people than ever want that lifestyle and the desire never seems to dull or go away. It only intensifies with each new generation, it seems.

And here's another thing they don't teach you in history class: once you've arrived on top and survey your surroundings, it can be a very lonely place. By the time you get there, you can be drained by what it took: the wear and tear on your body (often helped along by drugs and alcohol), and shedding important things in your life like friends, family, moral values, and mates.

You realize the only way out is down, and you can see a long line of people waiting to take your place.

When you're hot, everyone wants a piece of you. When you're yesterday's news, no one cares because there is new talent to be exploited and you are dead weight. It's like being the fastest gun in the West—someone always wants to take your spot. Now you're a target to be beaten. Just ask Jesse James, "Wild Bill" Hickok, or John Lennon. All of them were murdered by nobodies who wanted to become somebodies. James' killer, Robert Ford, was a small-time wannabe outlaw and earned a living for years portraying the assassination on stage. Ironically, ten years later, Ford suffered the same fate when he was shot in the neck at his tent saloon in Colorado. His killer became known as "the man who killed the man who killed Jesse James."

French novelist Victor Hugo said this type of competition and conflict is inevitable with fame: "Fame—and the money that comes with it—draw unpredictable situations and strange people. Fame must have enemies, as light must have gnats."

Sometimes the dark side of fame isn't the bad reviews, mean tweets, or jealous friends. It's what people thrust on you. If only you'd done this in that game. If only you'd change your appearance. If only you'd be nicer/quicker/meaner/

more melodious. According to your critics and fans alike, you must be this, that, or the other thing.

Here's another piece of bad news: it's never going to go away. Henry Winkler will always be "The Fonz." Anthony Michael Hall will stay thirteen for the rest of his life. And Molly Ringwald will forever be in Saturday detention. You do not escape fame. You will never be that person you were before. And you are not always afforded respect if you're famous: "Man, you look terrible. You don't look like you did in your hit movie" (even though it was thirty years ago), or "You've gained weight since your first playoffs" (back when you were twenty-one).

The Internet does not help by preserving every picture ever taken of you, whether at a movie premiere, in concert, or with a mouthful of food. You will never not be famous again. You could be broke, living in a rundown trailer park, or have not made a meaningful film in twenty years because Hollywood has deemed you box-office poison . . . but you'll always be famous.

There are two ways to go down the path: the slow death, like I just described, or the swift fall, which will take you out of the game almost instantly. When actress Winona Ryder was arrested for shoplifting in Beverly Hills in 2001, a powerful attorney got her sentence reduced to probation and a $2,700 fine. However, she was placed in Hollywood "jail" for almost twenty years. Ashlee Simpson's singing career crashed and burned in one night when it was discovered she lip-synced on *Saturday Night Live.* Cyclist Lance Armstrong fell hard when it was discovered he had been taking performance enhancing drugs. He was permanently banned from cycling and other athletic events, not to mention untold millions in endorsements. Baseball Hall of Famer Pete Rose also got a lifetime ban from the league for gambling on games while he managed the Cincinnati Reds.

Darryl Strawberry experienced the slow death. He was suspended from baseball three times, but luckily was never banned for life. He lost his status, his fortune, his good name, and almost his soul.

But by God's grace, he got called back to the big leagues a few years later.

This time it didn't matter how many homers or RBIs he hit. All that mattered was that he stepped up to the plate again.

FIVE

A MAN FOR ALL SEASONS

D arryl Strawberry was one of the most recognized names and brightest stars in professional sports in the latter part of the 20th century. As an eight-time all-star for the New York Mets, Los Angeles Dodgers, and New York Yankees, he naturally grabbed a lot of headlines for his prowess on the baseball diamond.

He also made the news for his off-the-field antics.

The man with the cool last name and the smooth left-handed swing was one of the game's best power hitters, and played a part in four world baseball championships. Strawberry hit an impressive 353 home runs[3] and had more than 1,000 RBIs over a seventeen-year career, which started in 1983. He could have achieved so much more had he not allowed drugs

---

3   MLB 107th all-time leader

and alcohol to sabotage his career. His descent into addiction led to long drug binges in crack houses, emotional wounds that took decades to heal, self-loathing over his actions, and running away from his responsibilities. These trials and tribulations resulted in three suspensions from Major League Baseball, incarceration, financial devastation, separation from family members, and thoughts of suicide. Many said that his God-given talents and gifts were wasted on Strawberry's lackadaisical attitude toward the game.

As one reporter wrote, "What he didn't achieve in baseball was more the story of Darryl Strawberry's career than what he actually accomplished."

I'm glad I didn't know *that* Darryl Strawberry. I can assure you the old Darryl Strawberry is dead and the one that has replaced him is a strong and mature Christian man whose every fiber is dedicated to the Lord Jesus Christ. I first met Darryl when many faith leaders were invited to a meeting at the White House. None of those leaders made an impression on me as much as Darryl did. We struck up a fast friendship, and he has been a guest at our church several times to talk publicly with me about his life, career, and faith.

In those conversations, Darryl revealed that he was raised by a Christian mother and a physically and emotionally abusive father, who in Darryl's words was "a raging alcoholic." Sadly, Darryl's father never showed or told his son that he loved him, never offered any fatherly support or guidance, and said he'd never amount to much. I can tell you from experience that those wounds are easily carried into adulthood. When Darryl stepped out onto the field at Shea Stadium in a Mets uniform as a twenty-one-year-old rookie, he could still hear his father's voice tell him,

"You're no good. You'll never amount to anything.

Even the roar of the crowds and the fact that he won the National League Rookie of the Year in 1983 could not drown out his father's negative voice.

Add fame to the mix and, well, you've got serious trouble.

Darryl said everything was available to him once he became a sports celebrity: money, homes, cars, adoring fans, and all the trappings of fame. He couldn't go anywhere without being recognized or hounded for his autograph. His life was no longer the same. The star treatment seemed nice on the outside, but he didn't like the fact that everyone seemed to want a piece of him. Notoriety, he felt, was an intrusion, and no one was there to teach him how to handle it. Darryl felt that all this led to personal regression and that his growth as a human being slowed to a stop. He had trainers to treat his aches and pains, an agent to negotiate his contracts, lawyers to get him out of jams, and hangers-on ready to fulfill all of his other needs. "They're all yours," Darryl told himself.

"You can indulge yourself without limits, without restrictions, and without responsibilities."

At the beginning of Darryl's career, he was an iron horse, swatting homers, catching fly balls on the run, stealing bases, and making it all look so incredibly easy. Darryl became the first National League player voted to the All-Star Game in each of his first four seasons.

There are athletes who thrive on being the greatest of all time and routinely breaking records, but that wasn't Darryl's personality or personal ambition. He just wanted to play ball and see where it took him. But between the media scrutiny, partying with his teammates, and the prying eyes of the public, that was easier said than done. Darryl was under tremendous pressure by owners, the media, and fans to lift his team to a pennant. But the Mets weren't quite there yet. Second place wasn't good enough in the Big Apple, and everyone let Darryl know what was expected of him after his sensational rookie year. All that pressure meant Darryl had to find a way to unwind after a game.

"Our way to wind down was drinking, drugging, gambling, and fornicating," Darryl said. "We were bad enough before, but '86 was the season when our lifestyle got way out of hand."

Beer was the foundation of their alcoholic lifestyle, Darryl said. They drank it in the clubhouse, on the plane, in the bus, even when they were being interviewed by newspaper reporters. It was always nearby and close at hand. Darryl even joked that in his heyday, the team hauled around more Budweiser than the Clydesdales.

But beer was not the only alcoholic beverage on the menu. Darryl and his teammates also drank rum, martinis, and threw back plenty of tequila shots. When they ventured into Manhattan for a night on the town, hitting some of the tonier nightclubs, the nose candy came out. And it wasn't done in the shadows or in a bathroom stall. There were mountains of it served on silver platters right next to the hors d'oeuvres.

These guys were like movie stars, rockers, and rappers all rolled into one, according to Darryl.

"Life was like one long buffet table laid out with vices and temptations," he recalled. "We were young, healthy, on top of the world, and very full of ourselves."

"Resisting temptation and vice was the last thing on our minds. We dove in headfirst."

Despite the two-fisted drinking and party-till-you puke attitude, the rough and tumble '86 Mets were not to be denied. When they beat the Houston Astros for the National League Championship, the team boarded a chartered DC-10 jet back to New York. On board, cases of champagne were consumed, mountains of cocaine were snorted in the lavatory, an *Animal House* inspired food fight erupted, players broke seats to convert them into beds, and the interior of the cabin was trashed to the tune of tens of thousands of dollars. Three people had to be carried off the plane upon exit due to consumption.

The team still had enough fuel in the tank to beat the Boston Red Sox in a seven-game World Series matchup. When it was all over, the Mets received a parade down Broadway in Manhattan. It was there that the mayor, the ever-colorful Ed Koch, gave them all keys to the city, dignitaries made speeches about how much the team meant to the city, and two million baseball-crazed fans showed their appreciation. For Darryl, the climb to the mountaintop was the culmination of years of hard work, the fulfillment of a childhood dream for a boy who grew up in Crenshaw, California.

But the law of gravity declares that what goes up must come down. And it didn't take long for Darryl to come crashing down to earth.

The vices and temptations soon turned into addiction and enslavement. Admittedly, Darryl said he was a classic Jekyll and Hyde alcoholic. Sober, he was laid back and quiet. But with a few beers in his system, he was nasty, obnoxious, and his anger was quick to emerge.

> When he did speed, he was totally out of control.
> That's when his life began to spiral.

A paternity suit led to a divorce from his first wife, Lisa. Their separation was splashed on the sports headlines of many New York papers. A gun possession also landed him on the headlines and in jail. Upper management sent him to a rehab facility, the very same place his teammate Dwight Gooden had been to a few months before. He stayed clean and sober for a two-month period before alcohol started creeping back into his life. His play on the field had also diminished and his attitude grated on the team's management. Darryl eventually wore out his welcome in Gotham and was traded to the Los Angeles Dodgers in 1990. He said the move was like "jumping out of the frying pan and into the fire."

Having grown up in Los Angeles, Darryl wasn't an alien in a strange town. He knew where to find trouble but didn't need to waste his time looking. It soon found him. In 1991, he was introduced to crack cocaine. He took one puff and was instantly hooked. The intensity of the high took him to a place where he could escape his pressure-filled life for a little while. The relief, he soon discovered, was only temporary.

"All the fame, all the success, all the money in the world don't add up to a thing if you're hurting in your soul," he said.

"It does no good to have millions of people and all that press telling you who you are, when you haven't figured that out yet for yourself. And I still hadn't."

Darryl had just signed a $20 million contract, and he was absolutely miserable. He was still filled with anger, self-hatred, pain, and frustration. Like most addicts, he traded playgrounds but found the same problems still existed. He married again, to a nice lady named Charisse from Orange County. The problem was that he loved his drugging and drinking lifestyle more then he loved her. Darryl continued drinking and drugging.

Father Time began catching up with Darryl. With age, he became more injury prone. He hurt his back and underwent major surgery. Drugs and alcohol relieved the pain but nagging long-term ailments began to erode his physical and mental strength.

His tenure with the Dodgers was a bust, but things were about to get a whole lot worse.

In 1994, the Internal Revenue Service announced that it was investigating Darryl for tax fraud based on unreported income from autograph and memorabilia shows. Even though Darryl had accountants, they never paid the tax on the hundreds of thousands of dollars he made at these shows, which was mostly cash that went into his pockets. But the IRS had a proposal; if Darryl would give them the names of other MLB players who also participated, they'd go easy on him during sentencing. He refused and the IRS made him pay the price.

> They came after him with the full might of the government, and now he was in their doghouse to the tune of $1.3 million in back taxes.

He also found himself in a bad place with the Dodgers that same year. The injuries, the partying, the bad press, showing up late for practice, and a failed rehab attempt exasperated the franchise, who bought him out of his contract in May 1994 after four years of turmoil and trouble.

The San Francisco Giants eventually picked up the thirty-two-year-old Strawberry, but right away he got sidelined with bad news. After a strong start with the team, MLB went on strike and then the season was shut down. That same year, his fifty-five-year-old mother, Ruby, who was Darryl's light and foundation, was diagnosed with breast cancer. His world was rocked. More bad news followed in December: the IRS was formally charging him for felony tax evasion. As a result, he slipped back into addiction and "ran to the crack pipe." In January 1995, he tested positive for cocaine and was suspended from baseball for two months.

The Giants didn't want to hang around and wait for Darryl to get his act together. They let him go.

Yankee owner George Steinbrenner tendered a contract to Darryl despite the fact that many in the franchise did not want him, including manager Buck Showalter. Darryl spent a lot of time that year riding the pine, but he kept his mouth shut. He eventually went on to help the Yankees win three more championships.

It seemed like Darryl the veteran was finally coming around. He and his wife Charisse found a cozy home in Fort Lee, New Jersey, and settled down. They had a daughter named Jade, and Darryl stopped drinking and taking drugs. But his mother's terminal diagnosis and her declining health devastated him. He was there when she took her last breath, and he assured her that he would take care of the family. A God-fearing woman, Darryl's mother said to him shortly before her passing,

"You can ride, you can hide, but He's gonna get it out of you. You're gonna have to do what He has called you to do."

Darryl spent many days in bed after his mother's death, feeling as if he'd let her down and disappointed her. That sort of stress can trigger the body, and in 1998, Darryl was diagnosed with colon cancer. He had to undergo surgery twice to remove a walnut-sized cancerous tumor. To add insult to injury, Darryl missed the World Series. The Yankees, however, dedicated their victory to him.

The following year, while in training camp, Darryl was arrested for cocaine possession and given a four-month suspension from MLB. When he came back, he helped the Yankees win their second straight pennant with two homers and four RBIs in post-season play. Three months later, he tested positive for cocaine and underwent additional cancer surgery. Say what you will about Darryl, but he was clearly a survivor, a true warrior. And in time, he would become a warrior for Christ. But his addiction to drugs and alcohol would delay that relationship.

In March 2001, a four-day drug binge left Darryl in an emotionally fragile state and he was put on suicide watch. He was sentenced to two years in a drug treatment center in Ocala, Florida, but was eventually ejected for continually breaking the rules. For that, a judge gave him eighteen months in the Gainesville Correctional Institute, but Darryl was released after serving eleven months.

Darryl's woes put a major strain on his marriage to Charisse, who came to visit him only once while he was locked up. That left him to think a lot about how he had behaved and the choices he made.

When Darryl eventually got out in 2003, playing baseball was no longer an option. He was offered a job with the Yankees as a spring training instructor, but not as a player. Darryl Strawberry had finally come to the end of himself and realized that God still had a plan for him. Darryl and Charisse grounded themselves in a church, and his life was now centered around his faith and family. Pastors at surrounding churches asked him to come and speak to their congregations and give his incredible testimony.

Sadly, his tribulations were not over.

Darryl began experiencing money woes. With his playing days in the rearview mirror, he still maintained his high-rolling ways though he could no longer afford them. Money began to emerge as a serious issue between himself and Charisse, who had built a separate life for herself and the kids when Darryl was away in prison. The stress caused him to binge and bicker. The couple had grown so far apart that the two felt it was best they move forward with their lives without each other. Darryl was still in the recovery process when Charisse filed for separation, then eventually, divorce.

Darryl may not have believed it at the time, but God was saving his best for last.

He met Tracy Boulware at a Narcotics Anonymous recovery convention. Boulware, who hailed from the St. Louis area, had gotten straight a year earlier. She grew up Catholic but was reexamining her beliefs and had joined a Bible study a month before the convention. The two met just when she was beginning her faith journey. Tracy's dad, who was a baseball fan, warned her about Darryl's checkered past. Tracy felt it wasn't fair to judge a man on bygones. Besides, she was in love after getting to know Darryl through phone calls, correspondence, and texts. Darryl knew this was the real deal because there were no hidden agendas.

His fortune was long gone, and his prospects weren't looking very good either.

Old habits die hard.

Darryl would disappear for days at a time to get high. Even though he would make excuses, Tracy knew exactly what he was up to. She had been there and knew about deceitful behavior as a former drug abuser. Tracy was also familiar with the drug dens and crack houses where Darryl might be holed up, and she hauled him out of there many times. When he wasn't high, he was impressed by her fearlessness and stunned that she still loved him.

At Darryl's lowest point, she marched into a known drug house and cornered him. He felt shame and didn't want to go.

"Why don't you just leave me here and let me die?" Darryl asked her.

"You're just not that lucky," Tracy said fiercely. "God has a plan for you."

Talk about faith . . .

Darryl recalled, "There were a lot of times when everybody threw me away and said, 'Well, he's a loser.' But Tracy saw me as something God wanted to do inside of me and she didn't give up."

And neither did God.

Darryl spent many years running from God until one day he sucked in his last deep breath and stopped running. He finally found true redemption and restoration in Jesus Christ, and he has been transformed.

"All of life's answers are in the book [the Bible], but we're looking for them and search for it in the news and on social media, and that's all fake," Darryl said. "Notice how everyone runs to everything else but the Bible? The importance of my life being transformed was running to the Bible.

"You've gotta remember everybody is going to leave or forsake you, but Christ will never leave or forsake you."

I've witnessed the transformed Darryl Strawberry, and he's inspiring. I recently invited him as a guest speaker at a men's conference I hosted. I was struck by his godly wisdom and most especially by his humility. Darryl sat for hours signing autographs and speaking to fellow Christians who wanted their moment with him.

Darryl stayed and talked and shared stories of his life until the last person left.

No one was turned away. That, to me, shows the real man behind the celebrity—a man who has had it all, lost it all, and came back to help others when the cameras have left and no one is keeping score anymore.

Today Darryl and Tracy live in a St. Louis suburb, where they have started Strawberry Ministries. They teach people how to grow in their faith and experience freedom in Christ through step-by-step resources and daily encouragement.

Darryl says that people can't be passive Christians and, to use a baseball metaphor, have to step up to the plate.

"Everybody wants the miracle of being what God wants him or her to be, but they don't want to do the work," Darryl said. "Discipleship is where you stir everything up, and that's where God gets to know you and He gets to have a relationship with you. You'll eventually find out who you are, and God's going to show you how He will use you. He's created us all for good and all we have to do is participate."

There are all-stars and there are MVPs, but Darryl Strawberry is both . . . a man for all seasons.

SIX

ALTER EGOS

Queen Elizabeth II is probably the only famous person in the 20th and 21st centuries who was genuinely herself all the time. She was born to a specific role, grew up with these expectations, understood them, and knew how to live with them.

Here's a funny anecdote that underscores my point: a few years before her death in 2022, she was in a store near her Scottish estate when she was approached by an excited older woman.

"You look just like the Queen!" the woman gushed.

"How reassuring," Elizabeth smoothly replied.

Most celebrities aren't that polished when it comes to switching their private and public personas. We'll never know in Queen Elizabeth's case because she wasn't the sort of person who would talk about it. Besides, we like our royalty at a distance and on a pedestal.

Celebrities are another story. Their favorite topic of conversation is usually themselves, so we have some insight there.

Public and private personas. What's the point? It can help people perform if they're shy or suffer from stage fright. That's the case with pop goddess Beyoncé. Early in her career she suffered from shyness. She wasn't super confident, fearless, or flirtatious. So, she created an alter ego for the stage and named her "Sasha Fierce." Sasha gave her the ability to power over cases of nerves and stage fright. Here's how Beyoncé put it:

"That moment when you're nervous, that other thing takes over for you."

When "Queen Bey" walked onstage, it wasn't her anymore. It was Sasha Fierce at the microphone. Eventually, she grew out of the crutch and didn't need Sasha to step in for her.

"Sasha Fierce is done. I killed her," Beyonce told *Allure* magazine in 2010. "I don't need Sasha Fierce anymore, because I've grown, and now I'm able to merge the two."

Psychologists called this mental trick of adopting an alter ego "self-distancing," a tool that helps people reason more objectively and see the situation from a slight distance. Beyoncé isn't the only one to employ to this tool. David Bowie is the most famous example of having adopted several alter egos during his lifetime. "Ziggy Stardust," the "Thin White Duke," and "Major Tom" were a few alternate Bowies.

"I think much has been made of this alter ego business," Bowie said. "I mean, I actually stopped created characters in 1975—for albums anyway."

Stars like Madonna, Bono, Garth Brooks, Lady Gaga, Nicky Manaj, Britney Spears, and even Snooki from MTV's *Jersey Shore* either have admitted or showcased their alter egos in their work.

"I think you see more of like, the party side of me, which I call 'Snooki,' it's kind of my alter ego," said Nicole Polizzi (Snooki's real name).

> An alter ego is a source of power as well as a shield.

It's much easier going onstage in a mask, it's even invisible to the audience. That's how it works for Britney Spears.

"I turn into this different person, seriously. Bipolar disorder," she said. "I'm tired of everybody touching me and things being plugged into my head."

Nicky Minaj's alter ego is an alpha male.

"Roman is my alter ego," Minaj said. "He's mean. He says the things I can't say."

Another demographic noted for having dual identities are superheroes. Peter Parker is Spider-Man. Bruce Wayne is Batman. Diana Prince is Wonder Woman. Bruce Banner is The Hulk. Tony Stark is Iron Man. And perhaps the most noted alter ego in comics is Superman's Clark Kent. But who is who? That's a question that has been explored in every one of these characters fictional lives. At one point or another, they've all rejected their other self whether it was the hero or the person. The other simply became too much because they were late for their wedding while saving the world or missed their parents last words for a similar reason. They wrestled with who came first or who should be put first. That's a question filmmaker Quentin Tarantino mulled over in Superman's case.

"Superman didn't become Superman. Superman was born Superman. When Superman wakes up in the morning, he's Superman. His alter ego is Clark Kent," Tarantino said. "Clark Kent is how Superman views us. And what are the characteristics of Clark Kent? He's weak . . . he's unsure of himself . . . he's a coward. Clark Kent is Superman's critique on the whole human race."

Real life can mimic the comics without the costumes.

Ask many a Hollywood tough guy or dashing leading man. Cary Grant was born Archibald Alec Leach in Bristol, England in 1904. He was an insecure, working-class man from a rough background, but acting gave him a way to become something he wasn't. On screen, Grant was known for being suave, debonair, and sophisticated, but that was a highly developed persona that took years to perfect. He admitted as much.

"I pretended to be somebody I wanted to be until, finally, I became that person," Grant said.

"Or he became me. Or we met at some point along the way." Grant changed himself and put that into roles, which became his hallmark. It was half-acting and half self-improvement. So, do actors have alter egos? Good question. They can disappear into roles. Some disappear so deeply and so deftly they truly become someone else.

The most famous example of that is a recent one.

When Heath Ledger took on the role of the Joker in 2008's *The Dark Knight*, he went deep. Some say too deep.

Before filming, Ledger locked himself up in a London hotel room for an entire month and maintained a diary to prepare for becoming the character. He experimented with voices, facial tics and possible backstories, and used Malcom McDowell's character in *A Clockwork Orange* as inspiration. He later described the role as "physically and mentally draining." The Joker, he said, was "an absolute sociopath, a cold-blooded, mass-murdering clown."

Six months after the movie was released, Ledger died of an accidental overdose.

His family was familiar with how he prepared for his roles, but when his father read the Joker journal, he said, "It was on a whole new level."

Actor Daniel Day Lewis, considered by many critics to be one of the finest thespians in the world, is also noted for completely disappearing into his roles. He learned Czech for *The Unbearable Lightness of Being*. He spent the entire shoot for *My Left Foot* in a wheelchair. In Michael Mann's *The Last of the Mohicans*, Lewis lived in the Alabama wilderness where he learned to hunt, track, and skin animals. He also picked up a new trade: building wooden canoes.

"I suppose I have a highly developed capacity for self-delusion, so it's no problem for me to believe that I'm somebody else," Lewis said.

For actor Peter Sellers of *Pink Panther* fame was a disaster unless he was on a movie set where he could disappear into one of his many iconic roles. Sellers was described by a biographer as a chameleon but a "sad, empty vessel." On screen, he was pure comic genius, but in his personal life, he was highly private and compartmentalized. No one ever got to see the whole man, with the exception of his four wives, who say he was controlling, complicated, and suffered from bouts of depression and paranoia. He also abused drugs and alcohol.

A *Today Show* reporter astutely picked up on the fact that Sellers lived a bifurcated life when he was promoting his last film, *Being There*. She wondered on air if there was "no Peter Sellers?" Sellers answered that it wasn't *quite* true.

However, behind the mask, he admitted to being an empty vessel.

"There is no me," he once joked on *The Muppet Show*. "I had it surgically removed." One wonders if he was really joking.

Let's face it: everyone is tempted to live a double life. The Bible warns against this.

It specifically states that if we have one foot in the world and one foot in Him, we will perish. James 1:8 says that a double-minded person is unstable in everything they do. James 4:8 says, "Come near to God and he will come near to you. Wash your hands you sinners, and purify your hearts, you double-minded" (NIV).

Jesus spoke out against the political leaders of his day, calling them out on their hypocrisy. Imagine what he'd have to say today to some of these slick politicians with their focus group-driven double-speak?

> Simply put, living a double life is a sin. The inside and the outside have to match.

Character is a direct reflection of our connection with God. He wants authenticity, not hypocrisy. It's essentially who you are when no one else is watching. That's your true self. That's the one God wants to know.

It took a long time for Vincent Furnier to figure this out. If that doesn't mean anything to you, it's because it's the name of an entertainer/businessman who enjoys golf, coaching kids' sports, doting on his grandkids, and regularly attending church. But that same man has another name—Alice Cooper.

Let's find out who he is . . .

SEVEN

ALICE UNCHAINED

Quick . . . what do you think of when I say the name Alice Cooper?

The guy with a woman's name wearing grotesque makeup? An "artist" who killed a chicken onstage during a concert? Rock and roll's boogeyman? A guy who belts out loud music with a huge boa constrictor draped around his neck? The godfather of Shock Rock? A cultural icon?

Would it surprise you to learn this Rock and Roll Hall of Famer is a Christian?

Let me correct myself—a shameless, outspoken, strong Christian.

I first met him in January 2019. I was preaching my usual Sunday sermon at the Harvest Orange County campus and spotted a recognizable couple sitting in the front row. They had never attended before, but I knew who they were. I also knew they were coming to our church. And they knew that I knew they were coming.

This lovely Christian twosome was Alice and Sheryl Cooper. Alice, of course, is the Rock & Roll Hall of Famer and Sheryl, a former professional dancer, is his wife of forty-five years.

Alice was not wearing black makeup or eyeliner. Nor was he carrying an eight-foot-long snake or swinging a saber. No top hat either. So, how did I know they were coming? Well, I admit it; I was tipped off.

Gabe Velasquez, a friend of mine, went to an Alice Cooper concert the night before and even managed to get backstage and speak to the showman. Alice mentioned that he and Sheryl liked to attend church whenever they were out on the road and were looking for a place to worship. Discussing convenient places of worship is not typical conversation backstage at a rock concert, but that tells you a lot about Alice. Gabe extended the offer to come to Harvest the following morning. They showed up. No entourage. No bodyguards. No reptiles. No pretenses. Just the two of them. They sat in the front row over to the side and no one bothered them. After the service, they came upstairs to my office to visit with Cathe and me.

My office is probably unlike any you have ever seen, especially for a pastor.

It's sort of a "man cave" meets serious library. Over my desk is a large photo of the Beatles that my son Christopher gave me. I have an original Beatles *Help!* poster and a Stingray orange crate bicycle hanging from my ceiling. It's similar to the one I used to ride as a boy. I have some surfboards mounted on the walls and a few guitars, including a replica of John Lennon's Rickenbacker that he played on *The Ed Sullivan Show*. I also have a poster of Billy Graham from the late '40s and busts of evangelists D. L. Moody and C. H. Spurgeon. Throw in some Disney memorabilia and you have a snapshot of my office. I forgot to mention I have a library with hundreds of books, mainly commentaries on the books of the Bible.

When Alice walked in, he looked around and the stories started coming.

He has personally met all the Beatles. He knew Jimi Hendrix, Janis Joplin, and Jim Morrison too.

When agent Shep Gordon was courting Alice as a client, he invited him to a hotel room filled with smoke and there in the flesh were Jimi, Jim, and Janis. Alice was impressed and signed with Shep immediately. Shep Gordon is still his agent more than a half-century later.

We found the Coopers extremely open and easy to talk to. So cool, so warm, and so friendly. Funny too. We are all about the same age, had the same cultural touchstones, and grew up liking many of the same things, including classic rock, guitars, and the faith that sustains us. On the latter subject, I did my best not to pry. Rarely do I ever stray into that territory with celebrities, often leaving it up to them exactly how much they want to reveal. But I could tell that Alice's faith was important to him. His and Sheryl's attendance that day after a big concert the night before spoke loudly. If you've never seen an Alice Cooper concert, rest assured that no one ever gets cheated. The energy he expends on stage is that of a man thirty years his junior, and when on tour, he does it five nights a week.

> The fact that he got up that next morning to go to church astounded me.

Our visit flew by, and at the end, we vowed to stay in touch.

A few months later, I emailed Alice to ask him if he'd be open to having a wide-ranging conversation on video, which ended up almost mimicking the conversation we had that day in my office. I figured if we could get that on tape, we'd be gold.

Alice said he'd be happy to oblige if I came to Phoenix where he and Sheryl have lived since the 1980s. We set up our interview to take place at his nonprofit foundation, Alice Cooper's Solid Rock Teen Center. The complex, which is the Coopers' gift to the community, inspires and challenges teens to embrace excellence and reach their full potential. Solid Rock offers free training in music, dance, sound and recording, lighting and staging, video production, art, and it provides a computer lab in a cool, supervised facility for teens to engage with their peers. At the start of the interview, Alice spoke about why he opened Solid Rock.

"I watched a couple of sixteen-year-old kids do a drug deal on the corner. I went, 'How does that kid not know he might be a great guitar player? Or that that other kid might be a drummer,'" he said.

"And it just struck me right then. Why don't we give them an alternative?"

The center took millions to launch, not to mention lots of elbow grease and hours upon hours of planning. And it's totally free to the teens who walk through the doors. You wouldn't blame them if they wondered if there's a catch or why Alice Cooper, who could be working on his golf handicap, does this.

"We're all a bunch of Christian guys here and the Lord told us to do it, so we just obeyed," he said with great humility. "So that's all."

That's all?

Alice's commitment to his fellow man and willingness to submit to the Lord is so simple, yet inspiring.

This place has become precious to him, and I can see why. He's offering a safe haven for young people and offering them a place where they might develop a hidden talent. He wants to expand to more locations in the Phoenix metro area and throughout the state in places like Tucson, Casa Grande, and Flagstaff. It's actually not unlike "seeding" a startup church.

You may be surprised to hear this, but Alice's roots are in the church. His grandfather was an evangelist, and his father was a part-time pastor.

Alice grew up knowing who the Lord was, but when he discovered Elvis Presley, the Beatles, and rock and roll, it took his focus away from Christ.

Vincent Damon Furnier was born on February 4, 1948, at Saratoga Hospital in Detroit. The hospital was located on the east side of the city and just south of Eight Mile Road. Cooper said "Butcher's Palace" was the hospital's nickname, "because not everyone came out in one piece." However, he fared well compared to some of the other infants. He was born with eczema and infantile asthma. He overcame the first ailment. The second one required a move to a more respiratory-friendly climate, so his parents pulled up stakes and moved to the San Fernando Valley in California. There his father, Ether Moroni Furnier, found work as an engineer at the Jet Propulsion Laboratory in Pasadena while his mother, Ella, took a job waitressing at Lawry's on La Cienega Boulevard. Young Vince spent a lot of his free time at one particular movie theater, which showed eight hours of horror movies in succession every Saturday. Predictably, this obsession lasted for several decades, fermenting like bad apple cider. When Vince became "Alice Cooper" (the name evolved from a three-week brainstorming session), his act looked like a horror movie with writhing snakes, electric chairs, fake blood, cut-up doll toys, and—best of all—having his own head cut off by a guillotine and then finishing the number.

> It was all an act of course, but it entertained his audience of young people and outraged their parents. Mission accomplished.

The move to Los Angeles coincided with his parents' attendance at church and embracing of the Church of Jesus Christ. It changed all of their lives, especially Ether. He gave up his three-packs-a-day smoking habit, cleared out the liquor cabinet, and cleaned up his language. The family was in church every Sunday, Wednesday, and Friday. On Saturdays, the Furniers cleaned the church for the next day's services.

"The Church was suddenly everything to us: A religion, a social life, a new family," Alice said.

"My father's devotion was inspiring. It affected my mother so deeply that within a month she stood up in church one day and asked to be baptized. My father did the same thing a few weeks later, and after that, our lives changed completely."

Ether Furnier was ordained in 1961 when Vince was thirteen. That was the same year the Furniers moved to Arizona, and the same year Vince almost lost his life. Two months after they moved to Phoenix, Vince got violently ill after eating lasagna. It was chalked up to the fact that his stomach couldn't handle spicy foods. Later, his parents found him passed out in a pool of vomit in his bedroom. They rushed him to the hospital.

Doctors opened Vince up and discovered his insides were riddled with peritonitis. His appendix had burst a few days before and every internal organ had been affected. The doctors extracted four quarts of poison from Vince's system, then sewed him up, stuck draining tubes in him, and pumped him full of morphine. They also told Ether and Ella their son had a ten percent chance of survival and to prepare themselves for the inevitable. The Furniers' instinct was to put on their spiritual armor and go to battle for Vince.

"My parents sat by my bedside and read the Bible and comic books to me: 'This sickness is not unto death but unto the glory of God.' I looked like I was ready for Hitler's ovens," Alice said. "I dropped almost half my weight—weight that I was never to recover. I reached a low of sixty-eight pounds. A call for help went out to church members and believers around the country. In Los Angeles the church people who ordained my dad prayed and fasted for me. Letters and cards arrived to the hospital by the dozens while my parents waited for the end to come. I can't offer any explanation as to why I lived except that it was a miracle. There is no doubt about it. It was a miracle that I pulled through, thanks to Jesus and the church and the faith of everyone around me."

"Why would the Lord save the life of Alice Cooper?"

The answer to that question would not be revealed for a few decades.

A few years after that frightful episode, Vince had an ordination of his own. A quartet from Liverpool, England, had invaded our shores in 1964 and appeared on a television variety hour called *The Ed Sullivan Show*. Vince, along with seventy-three million other Americans, tuned in to watch these four "mop-tops" perform their incredibly catchy songs, which instinctively made young girls lose their minds.

It changed the course of his life.

"The Beatles were like from another planet with the long hair and strange accents, but they were funny," Alice said. "They had a great sense of humor. The girls loved them, which immediately got our attention."

What Alice said is what I've heard literally thousands of other musicians state over the years—that the Beatles inspired them to pick up an instrument and play music for a living. As a music fan, I have developed an innate appreciation of musicians and artists, and in turn, totally respect their passion, dedication, and the hours they spend on their craft.

It was truly a special decade for music. In addition to the Beatles, on any given day, the radio blasted artists like Bob Dylan, Aretha Franklin, the Rolling Stones, the Beach Boys, Led Zeppelin, the Who, the Byrds, Jimi Hendrix, Cream, the Doors, Janis Joplin, Sly & the Family Stone, Jefferson Airplane, and also Motown, which offered a different type of sound. The music was fun, uplifting, challenging, psychedelic, and dramatic. It was truly the soundtrack to a historic decade.

By now Vince was a class clown and jock who ran track at Apollo High School, which then was at the northern edge of the city. He was also a gifted mimic who could imitate Barney Fife, Inspector Clouseau, or Stan Laurel with great ease. He had a natural magnetism that easily drew people to him.

"I went out of my way to be charming and funny in the classroom," he said.

"Not wise-guy funny, but nice funny. And I was known as a great diplomat. I could talk my way out of any fight, and I could talk my way out of just about any situation that came up."

That was a notion seconded by his best friend and fellow bandmate, Dennis Dunaway. He said Vince could talk to anyone about any topic and could quickly figure out what the other person wanted to hear and then say it. He had an unlimited repertoire of tales, some of them tall, according to Dunaway. He said Vince was smart, witty, hip, and was quick to laugh, especially at himself. Art class is where the two teens bonded and ultimately decided to become rock stars.

The Beatles inspired them to take that first step, and the decision was later solidified by Chuck Berry, Duane Eddy, and the Rolling Stones. But it was the Yardbirds that really put their musical imprimatur on Vince and the classic lineup of the Alice Cooper Band, which was their official name starting in April 1968. They included: Dennis Dunaway (bass), Michael Bruce (guitar), Glen Buxton (guitar), and

Neal Smith (drums). Between 1969 and 1973, they released seven studio albums and a string of hits ("Eighteen," "School's Out," "Billion Dollar Babies," and "No More Mr. Nice Guy") that changed rock music forever with their signature sound, a theatrical surrealistic stage show, and Alice's over-the-top, horror-inspired persona.

Critics tend to give the nod to the Rolling Stones, Led Zeppelin, the Who, Three Dog Night, or the Bee Gees for being the biggest bands of the 1970s, but they often forget to mention the Alice Cooper Band in the same breath. Their 1973 tour in support of the album *Billion Dollar Babies* not only shattered all previous box-office records previously held by the Rolling Stones, but it defined the modern era of touring. It was a world of jets, limousines, and champagne now, and Alice and his band of musical brothers chugged, snorted, inhaled, imbibed, ripped, tripped, and tweaked on all the "Satan's candy" they could lay their hands on. And being a stadium act who traveled by jet, that was a lot.

All the while, Alice's popularity shot through the stratosphere, especially after "The Chicken."

"The Chicken" is one of rock's most memorable moments. It's right up with Hendrix setting his guitar on fire, Pete Townshend smashing his guitar, or Ozzy Osbourne biting the head off of a bat. During the band's performance at the

Toronto Pop Festival in June 1969, a fan tossed a live chicken on stage. Alice saw the chicken and tossed it back into the audience. "It's a bird," he thought at the time. "It'll fly away." It did not. It was torn to shreds by the fans. However, the rumor that made the rounds was that Alice ripped the head off the chicken and drank its blood.

Alice never denied it—the story was too juicy and did wonders for his street cred.

But back to the pertinent question: exactly why was Alice Cooper so popular? He wasn't exactly everybody's cup of tea, especially where it concerned mainstream America. He and the band zigged when everybody else zagged.

He was different and not always likeable. And that was just fine by him.

"Rock was looking for a villain, and I was more than happy to be Captain Hook to everybody's Peter Pan," Alice told me in our conversation at Solid Rock.

And it worked like a charm. Alice said that once the band had a hit (they had fourteen Top 10 singles and a slew of gold and platinum albums), it was a "Willy Wonka golden ticket" to everywhere, especially Hollywood. It even got him a ticket to the Friars Club of Beverly Hills where all the comedians and entertainers whom he loved and adored as a kid accepted him into their tight-knit world. Groucho Marx went to a show and deemed that Alice's live act was simply an updated version of vaudeville, which was his entrée into this exclusive boys' club.

"I was the only rock star allowed into the Friars Club," Alice said in amazement. "There was Sinatra over there, and there was Dean Martin and Jerry Lewis over there . . . Bob Hope, Milton Berle, Steve Allen, Jimmy Durante, Sid Caesar, Johnny Carson, Sammy Davis Jr., and all the great comedians that I adored."

"They're all wearing black tuxedos and I'm in black leather. They just totally accepted me. 'Hey Coop, how are you?'"

Alice appeared on talk shows, hung out with big celebrities, old and new. He even hosted *The Muppet Show*. He was invited by Elvis to Las Vegas, went with Salvador Dali to New York's Studio 54, and hung out with Andy Warhol at the Factory. Because somehow hanging out with Frank Sinatra and Dean Martin wasn't enough, he formed the Hollywood Vampires, a celebrity last-man-standing drinking group comprised of Ringo Starr, Keith Moon, Harry Nilsson, Bernie Taupin, and Mickey Dolenz. When John Lennon was on his "Lost Weekend" in LA, he was deemed an honorary member, though he didn't do much standing. He was mostly wobbly-kneed around these world class carousers who occupied a loft inside the Rainbow Bar & Grill on the Sunset Strip.

How'd they get that unforgettable nickname?

"People started calling us the Hollywood Vampires because we'd never see daylight," he said. "We figured instead of drinking the blood of the vein, we were drinking the blood of the vine."

Alice Cooper had transcended the role of rock star to infiltrate American popular culture in music, movies, television, art, and the party scene.

But behind the scenes, not everything was as it appeared to be.

Alice was unraveling.

It started with beer. Alice drank it like a rock star. Lots of it. It even became a prop of sorts. At his alcoholic peak, he estimates he drank a case a day. That's a lot for a guy who barely weighed 140 pounds, if that.

He laughed it off. He told a reporter in 1973 that he started before breakfast and kept at it all day.

"Beer puts you in a good state of mind," he said. "You don't get drunk on beer, just sort of permanently high." A few years later, beer wasn't cutting it any longer; he graduated to whiskey and cocaine . . . then rock cocaine.

Alice had plenty of cautionary tales to show him not to go down that rock and roll highway. He knew Brian Jones, Jimi Hendrix, Janis Joplin, and Jim Morrison. Alice outdid them all in terms of abuse, which is saying a lot. That's an all-star list of heavy hitters.

But no one on earth can sustain that forever.

The first sign of the end came when Alice started vomiting blood every morning.

His doctor said that if he stopped drinking, he could probably record twenty more albums. But if he didn't, in two weeks he'd be jamming with his friends Jim Morrison and Jimi Hendrix in the afterlife.

"I didn't realize that I was an alcoholic until I realized that the alcohol was not fun for anyone," Alice said. "It was medicine."

The rocker checked into a sanatorium in New York. It was not a six-figure country club rehab center with handholding, day spa privileges, shopping trips, or horse therapy. Those kinds of places didn't exist back then. This was a place where the patients were often people who shook uncontrollably unless they had a whiskey first thing.

Wet brain, a disorder related to an acute vitamin deficiency, was common. It's a predictable complication of long-term heavy drinking combined with poor nutrition. If you live on a daily diet of Maker's Mark, Winstons, and cocaine, and eat pancakes once every three or four days, you're going to get it. Wet brain can lead to irreversible confusion, difficulty with muscle coordination, and even hallucinations.

That's what Alice spent three months with at the end of 1977.

He got clean and sober, but it didn't last long thanks to freebase cocaine appearing on the scene. It's pure cocaine. And there's never enough because it's so addictive. Chicken scratching the carpet at four in the morning for that rock you're sure bounced off the mirror is a reliable sign you're off the rails. Whatever doesn't kill you makes you sleep until three in the afternoon.

Many artists who used it went off the deep end for a few years—Alice included.

Starting in the 1980s, he recorded a string of what he called "blackout albums" that vacillated from rock to synth-laden new wave to hard-nosed punk. Alice didn't remember writing these "trippy songs," recording them, touring them, or how he made it out of bed most afternoons, despite the fact he had a loving and supportive wife in Sheryl and a newly born daughter, Calico, to live for. He was skeletal and pale looking, having lost a lot of weight from not eating or sleeping. The freebase also aged him significantly.

Years later he described his emaciated appearance as a "soldier of fortune that's on meth and he's capable of killing anybody."

The only person Alice was killing, however, was himself.

In the fall of 1983, his family checked him into the hospital, where he was diagnosed with cirrhosis of the liver. During his two-and-a-half-week stay, he was nursed back to health on a steady diet of vitamins and nutritional food. But a lot of damage was done to both his body and his marriage.

Sheryl said she could no longer watch him commit slow-motion suicide and moved out of their LA residence with Calico. They headed to Sheryl's hometown of Chicago. She filed for divorce in 1983. He said it was the lowest point of his life, but the cocaine was speaking a lot louder than Sheryl at that point. One morning, shortly after Sheryl and Calico left, he crawled out of bed and looked into the mirror. He was horrified by what he saw.

"It looked like my makeup, but it was blood coming down," Alice told me.

"I went to the bathroom and flushed the rock down the toilet and went to bed for three days. I woke up and called her and said, 'It's done.' She said, 'You have to prove it.' And that was the beginning of our relationship coming back."

It was also the beginning of his relationship with Christ coming back. As the son of a pastor and grandson of an evangelist, Alice knew who the Lord was. He'd simply been distracted by everything that had happened since he formed his band in his teens.

Now, like the prodigal son, he was ready to come home.

One of their provisos for getting back together in mid-1984 was that they start going to church. They moved to Arizona and attended a large church in North Phoenix, which had a membership of 6,000 people.

The prodigal son had returned home and allowed himself to be embraced by his fast-approaching Father once again.

"I got to a point where I was tired of this life. I knew who Jesus Christ was, and I was denying Him because I was living my own life, and I was living my life without Him," Alice said. "I knew that there had to come a point where I either accepted Christ and started living that life or, if I died in this world, I was in a lot of trouble. And that's what really motivated me . . . When the Lord opens your eyes and you suddenly realize who you are and who He is, it's a whole different world."

Alice's next leap of faith was getting baptized. He felt like a new creature in Christ and wanted to put "Alice" to rest once and for all.

His pastor, a very wise man, didn't think that was such a good idea.

"I went to my pastor and said, 'I think I got to quit being Alice Cooper,'" he recalled. "And my pastor goes, 'Really? You think God makes mistakes? Look, He put you in the exact camp of the Philistines now. So, what if you're "Alice Cooper" now? What if you're following Christ *and* you're a rock star, but you don't live the rock star life? Your lifestyle is now your testimony.' And that made total sense to me, you know?"

The newly sober rock star had a son in 1985 (Dash) and a second daughter (Sonora) in 1992. His family expanded once again in 2012. That's when he opened the doors to the original Solid Rock Teen Center in Phoenix. Built in partnership with Genesis Church, the center was fully functional after more than a decade of detailed planning and fundraising.

In 2021, he opened a second center in Mesa, Arizona, in partnership with Mesa Public Schools.

Almost thirty years after surrendering his life to Christ, Alice said dealing with Alice Cooper is no longer an issue, nor is he the top priority in his life.

"You take care of your relationship with God first, then you heal your relationship with your wife, certainly your kids. And now Solid Rock is a very big part of my life. Alice Cooper is somewhere like five or six in terms of importance," Alice said. "To me, the funniest and oddest thing is this character that I used to be [Alice Cooper]. They used to tear my albums up on *The 700 Club*. Now he's an agent for Christ. And what a miracle that is! You know, and I'm still Alice Cooper. I'm still playing this dark character, but he's now an agent of Christ. Yeah, very weird."

It's not weird to me. I've seen many instances where God can take anyone who is willing to submit to Him and transform them into a messenger of grace and hope. God can and does work miracles in people's lives all the time. Heaven is not going to be filled with perfect people, just forgiven people. We simply have to admit our sin and turn from our old ways. The Bible even says,

> "If we confess our sins to him, he is faithful and just to forgive us our sins and to cleanse us from all wickedness" (1 John 1:9 NLT).

God gives second, third, and fourth chances in life . . . amazing grace until we draw our last breath. Alice embodies this. He out-partied Jim Morrison, Janis Joplin, and Jimi Hendrix. That's worthy of some sort of twisted Grammy Award. He's played in front of millions of people. He was one of the top rock stars in the world in a time when rock stars were emperors with private jets and albums that sold in the multi-millions.

But in the end, he was humbled and alone, utterly naked before God like the day he was born.

God told Alice He wasn't done with him yet. There was work for him to do. And He sent the skinny rocker from Phoenix to do His will . . . to pay it forward.

God really does work in ways mysterious . . . to us.

But not to Him.

Afterword

According to several news reports and polls, approximately fifty percent of people want to be famous. Maybe even after you've read this book you fall into that big group of folks who long for notoriety and fame. Okay. Fine. Ambition can be an admirable trait and lead to great things, for oneself and sometimes for the greater good.

Even if you would really like to see your name in lights or plastered all over social media, this short book's message is that you, Beyoncé, Kim Kardashian, and Brad Pitt all have something in common. Your life will, someday, come to an end. All the wealth and influence and privilege in the world cannot deflect that day of reckoning. It's no news to you that you can't take it with you—not the $300,000 Italian sportscar that barely comes your knees, the mansion with the guitar-shaped pool, or the jet that can zip you around the world.

The four people chronicled in this book had all of that and more. But what ultimately fulfilled them was their relationship with Jesus Christ. Sometimes they didn't realize that until almost the end, when the fame and fortune were taken away or when they were staring death in the face.

Being famous sped Cash, Cooper, McQueen, and Strawberry to their mortal realization sooner than if they'd been mediocre, plunking their guitar or tossing their ball around on the weekends, like most of us do for fun. Their fame brought on the type of indulgence that few can afford. Our sinful natures will take us down the wrong road and crush our souls if temptation is as easy as putting out your hand and barking, "Diet Coke!" It's just not natural.

Someone has said, "It takes a very steady hand to hold a full cup."

It's almost impossible to keep a level head and maintain some kind of alignment when all you hear is how great you are. Or how much box-office you bring in. Or how many songs your fans download. Or how many fannies you put in the seats at the stadium. The problem with all these scenarios is that it all goes away eventually. New blood is always nipping at your heels, chewing on your pant leg. It's a stream that never ends. Do you see a shortage of kids who want to be rock stars, matinee idols, Instagram models, Social Media Influencers or pro ball players? Me neither.

The celebs all confess, when you're the one on top, you're the one they're gunning for. Actor, singer, and entertainer Kris Kristofferson once said, "The turkey with the longest neck is the one everyone is shooting at."

They stop shooting when you're old and scrawny and there's barely any meat on your bones.

At that point, no one really cares about you . . .
but God always will, no matter who you are,
what you've done, or where you are in your life.

My friend, Evangelist Billy Graham, touched on this subject in 2014 near the end of his life. He said, "Fame in itself isn't necessarily wrong if a person comes by it honestly and hasn't compromised his or her moral integrity . . . But I strongly urge you not to make this your goal in life. For one thing, you'll almost certainly be disappointed, because for every person who becomes a celebrity, thousands of others fail to reach that goal. Fame is also fleeting; today's celebrity is often forgotten in a few years."[4]

Fame is today's currency. Two millennia ago, Paul the Apostle warned his young friend Timothy that the love of money was the root of all evil (1 Timothy 6:10). This is still true. But now you can add, "the love of self and the passion

---

4   Billy Graham, "My Answer: Fame is fine, but faith is better," LA Times, August 8, 2014, https://www.latimes.com/socal/daily-pilot/opinion/tn-dpt-me-0809-billy-graham-my-answer-20140808-story.html.

for fame." They are right up there with it. Now, remember that these things are not inherently evil, but if you worship them, if they drive you, they will turn on you. Loving these things is not God's best for us.

Tragically, celebrity has even found its way into churches. Some leaders become so famous they rarely mix with the congregation. There is a hierarchy with VIP seating, restricted backstage access, and lavish green room spreads. When high-profile entertainers or sports stars attempt to sit with the main congregation, they are ushered to the front rows instead. I have to be on guard that this doesn't happen in my church. James wrote about this very thing a long time ago (see James 2:3).

It's not what Jesus would do either.

Jesus intentionally associated with the most unfortunate, like lepers, convicts, corrupt tax collectors, and other disreputable sinners.

Famous or not, there's a day when we are all welcomed into the house of the Lord, and God won't be asking for your backstage pass.

Heaven, you'll someday find, is the ultimate VIP lounge. That'll be the coolest place to hang out.

About the Authors

Greg Laurie is the senior pastor of Harvest Christian Fellowship, with campuses in California and Hawaii. He began his pastoral ministry at the age of nineteen by leading a Bible study of thirty people.

Since then, God has transformed that small group into a church of some 15,000 people. Today, Harvest Christian Fellowship is one of the largest churches in America and consistently ranks among the most influential churches in the nation.

In 1990 he began holding large-scale public evangelistic events called Harvest Crusades. Since that time, more than 10 million people have participated in these events in person or online around the United States. Harvest Crusades also have been held internationally in Canada, Australia, and New Zealand. More importantly, over 500,000 people have made professions of faith through these outreaches.

Greg is the featured speaker of the nationally syndicated radio program *A New Beginning* and also has a weekly television program on Lifetime, Fox Business, Newsmax, Daystar, the Trinity Broadcasting Network, and KCAL 9 Los Angeles.

Along with his work at Harvest Ministries, he has served as the 2013 Honorary Chairman of the National Day of Prayer and also serves on the board of directors of the Billy Graham Evangelistic Association. He holds honorary doctorates from Biola University and Azusa Pacific University.

He has authored over seventy books, including *Revelation: A Book of Promises*, *Billy Graham: The Man I Knew*; *Johnny Cash: The Redemption of an American Icon*; and *Steve McQueen: The Salvation of an American Icon*, and his autobiography, *Lost Boy*. Greg's favorite writing project is his work as general editor of the *New Believer's Bible*.

He also has produced a number of feature films and documentaries, including *Steve McQueen: The Salvation of an American Icon*, *A Rush of Hope*, *Johnny Cash: The Redemption of an American Icon*, and the story of his life is told in the feature film, *Jesus Revolution*.

You can follow Greg's preaching, teaching, and writing at harvest.org.

Greg has been married to Cathe Laurie for fifty years, and they have two sons: Christopher, who is in Heaven, and Jonathan, as well as five grandchildren.

Marshall Terrill is a film, sports, and music writer; journalist and author of more than thirty books, including best-selling biographies of Elvis Presley, Johnny Cash, Steve McQueen, and Billy Graham. He has also executive produced documentaries on Steve McQueen and Johnny Cash. He resides in Tempe, Arizona with his wife Zoe.

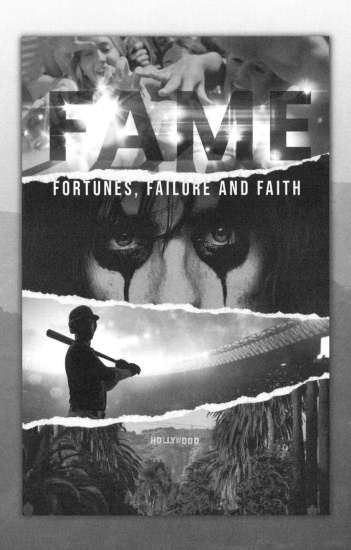

FAME

FORTUNES, FAILURE AND FAITH

Conversations with those who've been there, done that, and finally found what they were looking for.

WATCH AND LEARN MORE: HARVEST.ORG/FAME

OTHER WORKS BY
GREG LAURIE
AND MARSHALL TERRILL

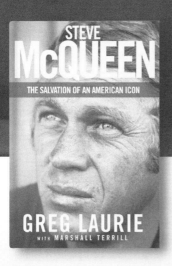

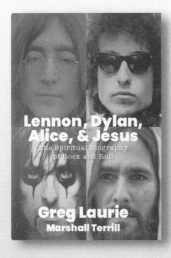

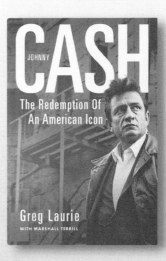

discipleship

**Connect with the
Harvest: Discipleship Platform
to fellowship with likeminded believers
and find valuable resources.**

**Grow with us at:
DISCIPLE.HARVEST.ORG**

Discover more at
harvest.org